A PATCHWORK OF FREEDOM

TRUE STORIES. SECRET QUILT CODE.
HOPE FOR TODAY.

Compiled and Edited by Lori Wagner

A PATCHWORK
OF FREEDOM

TRUE STORIES. SECRET QUILT CODE.
HOPE FOR TODAY.

A Patchwork of Freedom:
True Stories. Secret Quilt Code. Hope for Today.

Affirming Faith
1181 Whispering Knoll Lane
Rochester Hills, MI 48306
loriwagner@affirmingfaith.com
www.affirmingfaith.com
Printed in the United States of America.

Dedication

I dedicate this book to my firstborn daughter, Noelle, with a heart full of love and prayers that she would fly on freedom's wings and fulfill her destiny in God with joy.

TABLE OF CONTENTS

26. Lost Children: LaNaye Perkins – Olive Branch, Illinois
27. Basket: Debbie Roome – Christchurch, Canterbury, New Zealand
28. Maple Leaf: Karen Skolney – Kelvington, Saskatchewan
29. Butterfly: Bonnie Winters – Philipsburg, Pennsylvania
30. Bird in the Air: Anne Linington – Totland Bay, Isle of Wight, United Kingdom
31. Blazing Star of Kentucky: Cheryl Yates – Paducah, Kentucky
32. Going Around the Mountain: Bob and Linda Welch – Warren, Michigan
33. Shepherd's Crossing: Dorene Lilley – Rochester Hills, Michigan
34. Freedom: Jenny Teets – Farmingdale, New York
35. Nine Patch: Lori Rose – Buford, Georgia
36. Cumberland Gap: Claudette Walker – Oakland Township, Michigan
37. Ring of Roses: Lydia Gagoh – Rochester Hills, Michigan

FOREWORD

I love uncovering a mystery and learning new things. During my research for *Quilting Patches of Life*, I discovered information I found too fascinating to leave unexplored. It was a Civil War secret, so I dove in and began searching out a mysterious "Quilt Code" allegedly used in the Underground Railroad.

There has been controversy over the code's plausibility or accuracy. The purpose in writing this book is not to prove or disprove the theory. We cannot with absolute certainty validate or disclaim the possibility altogether. The nature of a secret is by definition secretive.

My purpose in writing *A Patchwork of Freedom* is to offer hope through the true stories of Christian men and women from around the world—stories of freedom experienced by others as they walked through the days and events of their lives. The connection of each story to a quilt pattern associated with the "Underground Railroad Quilt Code" and Civil War era adds dimension and spiritual application to the lessons shared I hope you enjoy.

Using a bit of poetic license and the "Quilt Code" premise, *A Patchwork of Freedom* pieces together scraps of testimonies and vignettes of emancipation to inspire you as you work through the patches of your life.

Thank you for reading. More information on the "Quilt Code" is available in the Resources/Notes section.

The "Underground Railroad Quilt Code"

"The monkey wrench turns the wagon wheel toward Canada on a bear's paw trail to the crossroads. Once they got to the crossroads, they dug a log cabin on the ground. Shoofly told them to dress up in cotton and satin bow ties and go to the cathedral church, get married, and exchange double wedding rings. Flying geese stay on the drunkard's path and follow the stars."

—Ozella Williams as quoted in the book *Hidden in Plain View*

CHAPTER 1
MONKEY WRENCH

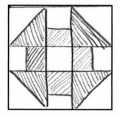

Val Mossop – Surrey, British Columbia

Depression invaded my life. It hovered constantly. I fought against it by every means I could think of, clueless to its origins. I knew I was blessed. God had given me a comfortable home, a faithful, loving husband, four children and a wonderful church. Above all, I had Jesus. He knew me and I knew Him.

Fighting depression on my own brought no results. Pushing it down, burying it, squashing all the negative feelings and memorizing Scripture did not help. I quoted the fourth chapter of Philippians often, especially verse eight, my favorite: "Finally brethren, think on these things..." I purposed to fill my mind with positive things. "I do think positively. I am doing it," I told myself, all the while silently screaming, not understanding why I felt no better and resenting the fact I did everything I knew to do with no relief.

A bout with cancer hammered my vulnerable veneer. Anxiety and the inability to concentrate made teaching impossible. Very involved and committed to my local church, my pastor's resignation added more stress—compounded by troubles in the lives of close family members. Tragic deaths of young acquaintances added to the mix, and finally my façade of "competent Christian" crumbled altogether.

In addition to emotional pain, I suffered physically. My doctor sent me from specialist to specialist. All found nothing wrong. One early summer day, while listlessly painting a short section of fencing in my yard, I mulled over thoughts of suicide. I felt myself slip into

11

dangerous territory. Thankfully, my faith kept me from following through, but I knew it was time to give up on my own remedies.

I sat in the doctor's office, rigid, scared and unsmiling, determined to find the key to unlock my emotional prison. "You have to think of something else," I begged him. "I can't stand the pain anymore."

"One can have depression because of sexual abuse in their childhood," the doctor said, "at an age they should be able to remember, but don't." The thought was incomprehensible, but at the same time, I could not deny the possibility. I felt nothing at his words, just hollow, numb. I am not sure I even gave a verbal response as I left his office.

A few days passed. I decided to take the doctor's advice and fill the prescription he wrote for antidepressants. Over the course of a few weeks, my thoughts became increasingly scrambled. I spoke with my doctor again and this time agreed to see a therapist.

Therapy was a monumental decision for me—one that created an even greater inner turmoil. In the early 1990s, solid Bible-believing churchgoers just did not need therapy, at least not in my area. Yet, with faith in Jesus, I continued down the path seeking help and healing.

I knew there must be a reason for my distress, and there had to be a way to work through it. Amidst the pain, I maintained a passion to be all I could in God. Looking back from the other side of healing, I know that was what God wanted too. God and I were inseparable partners through the longest, darkest valley in my life. He supplied the encouragement; I supplied the determination. Somehow, slowly but surely, I discovered the cause of my depression; but things got worse before they got better.

A barrage of intrusive flashbacks proved my doctor's diagnosis correct. Scenes of sexual abuse, animal torture, and severe psychological maltreatment invaded my thoughts and dreams. The memories did not come like ordinary recollections, but in the severe, ongoing emotional reactions of Post Traumatic Stress Disorder.

I experienced the memories in dissociated states. I found myself speaking to my therapist as a three year old on one occasion and an eight year old on another. Whatever the age I relived in my memories, I begged her in a small, pathetic voice not to hate me if I told her what happened.

The abuse extended over years, and therapy took longer than anticipated. Dissociative episodes also occurred outside the secure environment of my therapist's office. Everyday stress and noise caused adverse reactions. I ran out of church because the drums triggered some kind of fear. I was only able to work part time. Changing jobs became the norm and financial difficulties added to the turmoil in my family, all of us questioning why I was no better. At the time, as I walked through the fog and the pain, I did not realize my husband had taken over many of the household chores.

The road to recovery was long and difficult, but the Lord walked every step of the way with me and my family. During years of therapy, God strengthened us with specific scriptural promises. Early on, Psalm 66 assured that after everything, He would bring us out into a wealthy place. Although the passage was encouraging, it also warned that things would get more difficult before they improved. I knew I had to get to the bottom of the psychological hindrances before I could overcome them.

Prayer sustained me. Music gave hope. Many times, just when I needed it most, the worship leader would begin the song Beauty for Ashes (Isaiah 61:3), and my heart would be encouraged. Though not yet freed, I knew someday I would be released from the pain of the past.

Writing became one of the tools I used to retain my sanity—to release the inner tension when I felt I would explode with anxiety. I wrote to remind myself of God's goodness and blessings and because of a burning need to tell. I hoped someday to have the opportunity to encourage others walking through their own dark valleys.

Reconciling the past in light of the present has brought such freedom in God. Forgetting is an often-misunderstood word, especially when it comes to "...forgetting those things that are behind..." (Philippians 3:13). I could not just forget the past. I had to meet it, resolve the misunderstandings, purge the lies the enemy planted, and look at the past in the light of God's Truth.

Jesus is the Truth and Jesus prevailed in my life. In Him and through Him I am well and have come into that "wealthy place" of peace with God and my past. My family and I now celebrate the life of liberty God provides for whosoever will. Whom the Son sets free is free indeed.

❧ ❧

The Monkey Wrench quilt pattern, the first listed in Ozella William's "Underground Railroad Quilt Code" is said to have a dual meaning. The first refers to a specific person. The nickname "Monkey Wrench" was given to the most knowledgeable person on a plantation and usually referred to the blacksmith. Because of his position and skill, he was free to travel and move around without rousing suspicion, all the while communicating with people and passing information. A monkey wrench is also the name of a heavy metal tool used by blacksmiths.

Ozella Williams claimed this quilt pattern instructed those planning to escape to gather the tools and items needed in preparation for their journey. On a flight for freedom, physical tools would aid runaways along the way, as well as whatever provisions could be gathered and carried in a small bundle.

It is cliché, I know, but life really is a journey. Val's story lets us know that for some trips, people must gather provisions from outside sources to help them on their way. In Val's case, her bondage was not of her own making, as was the case of the enslaved in pre-Civil War America. The abuse forced upon Val as a child required that she, as an adult, take the initiative to obtain the help she needed on the path to healing and freedom.

Every one of us has experienced loss and disappointment. Life brings pain, and we all need help coping from time to time. While some of us have not suffered depression or abuse to the extent therapy or medication would be beneficial or required, others understand exactly where Val has been. And that is the beautiful part of her story. It's where Val has been— where she came from, not her destination, and not her life's story. This chapter is but a part of her story—a part that no longer paralyzes with pain or fear. She has a testimony to the overcoming power of God that freed her from a stricken heart to walk in newness of life.

CHAPTER 2
WAGON WHEEL

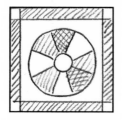

David E. Hepworth — Auburn Hills, Michigan

He was old. Of course, to a boy of fourteen, everyone seems old, but still, he was old—old and sad. All around him, families and couples vacationed on the bright summer afternoon in beautiful West Virginia.

Harper's Ferry, a town where history walks the streets, peeks around corners, and glances through windows at modern passersby, is a place haunted by bloody uprisings. In 1860, abolitionist John Brown stormed the federal armory attempting to rouse slaves to revolt. In 1862, a second conflict raged in conjunction with the bloodiest day in United States history, the battle of Antietam.

The year was 1972, and in the echoing shouts of rebellion long fought and settled, an old man wept. He sat on a bench with his shoulders slumped inside his tan sports coat. Weak, alone and dejected, he clung to his sole possession, a tweed valise resting on his lap.

My father, two brothers and I were in Harper's Ferry on a mission to explore the past. We came to discover the exploits of men, Northern brother against Southern brother, who believed in causes worth fighting for even at the expense of their lives. My brother, Roy, in particular, was fascinated with the Civil War. Maybe it was because he understood true courage, not of words, but of sacrifice.

Confined to a wheelchair his entire life, Roy's mobility came not from legs, but from wheels. And he could do amazing things with those wheels. Roy "ran" faster than I. He maneuvered curbs. He popped wheelies and flew down sidewalks at blinding speeds. No obstacle deterred him, except one. Roy was able to descend stairways bouncing down step-by-step, but he could not climb them.

Harper's Ferry was built into the Blue Ridge range of the Appalachian Mountains where the Potomac and Shenandoah rivers join. Surrounding the quaint town, beautiful cottonwoods, beech, and cedars blanket the mountains in blue-green silhouette. Cool breezes whistle through the valleys, and a unique elegance inhabits the area.

In 1783, Thomas Jefferson climbed the mountain behind the town and stood on a large rock overlooking the river and surrounding area. He later published his reflections, which gave that rock its name, Jefferson Rock. Since Jefferson's visit, people have traveled many miles to climb the trail and sit on the same rock, to see the beauty and hear bits of history flowing past in gurgling rivers.

We had come to this place with the intention of climbing the 300 small, slippery, twisted stairs up to the very spot Thomas Jefferson stood. No one was more eager than Roy. We had already determined to flip his chair backwards and pull him, step by step, up the mountain stairway. It was while we were contemplating how to do that we saw the old man.

My father studied him for a few moments and then quietly walked over. Dad, always massive in my eyes, seemed even larger towering over the slight figure. He joined him on the bench and extended his hand. Large, white and sausage-fingered, it dwarfed the old man's small, black, and fragile hand. "Is there anything I can do to help?"

"I have lived a long life," the old man began haltingly. "I have never traveled more than a few miles from my home. I read about this place many years ago—about Thomas Jefferson's description of its beauty and the war tearing that beauty apart." He stopped and took a deep breath, holding back a sob.

"I determined then that I would one day visit and climb the mountain all the way to the top to see Jefferson Rock. You can see four states at once from there, ya know," he said with a bit more excitement. Dad nodded.

"But I waited too long. I am finally here, with everything I own in this little case, but I am just too tired, too weak, and too old to climb to the top." The man shuddered, dejected. Tears tracked his dusty cheeks.

"It has been my life's dream to see the rock. If I could see it, then I could die happy, but I cannot." He withdrew a large red handkerchief from his pocket and wiped his eyes.

Dad, moved by the emotion in the man's voice, looked up at my brother and me with raised eyebrows. We understood his silent question. We understood the strong desire and determination we had seen mirrored so many times in Roy's life.

We took turns, my dad, brother, and I. First, two of us pulled Roy up in the wheelchair, then another placed the old man's arm around his shoulder and lifted him. We switched places so none of us would get too tired and step-by-step, rest-by-rest, we carried both: a young man whose legs were useless from birth, and an old man whose legs were useless with age.

Each new step brought discovery and revelation—new, uncharted regions where wheels had never been and remembrances of historic days past filled with federal troops and firing muskets. At each pause, the old man shared more of his life, what it was like growing up in the south. We talked about our experiences growing up in the north. Finally, shirts soaked with perspiration and faces flushed with exertion and revelry, we arrived at the summit.

In the old man, we saw joy and satisfaction; in Roy, pride and admiration. Here, where men had bled and died for causes greater than themselves, another battle had been waged and won. Though smaller, it bore its own significance: for a young man, knowledge that mountains cannot curb determination; for an old man, a tearing down of cultural divisions and the realization of a life's dream.

It has been many years since I stood, a boy of fourteen, looking up the weather-worn steps that lead to Jefferson Rock. Both the old man and my brother are gone. Thinking back to that experience, I find myself missing them both, each in their own way, but both for the lessons they taught me on a warm summer afternoon at a place called Jefferson Rock. It was a place where God used my Dad, brother and me to give "hinds' feet in high places" (Habakuk 3:19) to an old man and a boy who leapt with our aid over their obstacles to a place of victory.

According to the "Quilt Code, the Wagon Wheel pattern instructed potential runaways to pack provisions. They were to take only the essential items needed to survive, as if they were packing a wagon for a long journey.

A Wagon Wheel also symbolized a chariot, a means of deliverance. The spiritual, Swing Low Sweet Chariot, with its repeating phrase, "coming for to carry me home," was one of Harriet Tubman's favorite songs, one she used to send messages to those around her. Mrs. Tubman, one of the most famous conductors of the Underground Railroad, used familiar spirituals as signals to hiding slaves. The lyrics indicated whether runaways should remain hidden or take the next step on their journey to freedom. In addition to conveying messages, wagons with hidden compartments often transported runaways.

In David's story, the elderly man carried his life's possessions in one small case. He also carried a dream in his aged frame. Roy's "chariot" transported him from place to place, and he wheeled along a passion to reach for something beyond his grasp. Both men, young and old, faced obstacles they could not overcome on their own. In this touching story we see how God uses people like David, his father, and brother, to bring dreams to life for others. When Roy and the feeble man accepted sincere offers of assistance, they reached beyond their limitations and saw their dreams fulfilled, and it became a rewarding experience for all involved.

I pray that as we face the obstacles in our lives, our passion to overcome them will connect with God's provision. When we reach the end of our abilities, may we be open to the means God provides. In antebellum America, the Ohio River was commonly considered the Jordan River—the dividing line between North and South, slave states and free. When we are God's hands and feet, perhaps we become the "band of angels" referenced in *Swing Low Sweet Chariot*. May we be sensitive to the needs of others and help them cross their "Jordan Rivers."

Swing Low Sweet Chariot
I looked over Jordan and what did I see,
Comin' for to carry me home!
A band of angels comin' after me,
Comin' for to carry me home!

Swing low, sweet chariot,
Comin' for to carry me home!
Swing low, sweet chariot,
Comin' for to carry me home!

If you get there before I do,
Comin' for to carry me home,
Jess tell my friends that I'm acomin' too,
Comin' for to carry me home.

Swing low, sweet chariot,
Comin' for to carry me home!
Swing low, sweet chariot,
Comin' for to carry me home!

I'm sometimes up and sometimes down,
Comin' for to carry me home,
But still my soul feels heavenly bound
Comin' for to carry me home!

Swing low, sweet chariot,
Comin' for to carry me home!
Swing low, sweet chariot,
Comin' for to carry me home!

The African American registry records December 21, 1840, as the day *Swing Low Sweet Chariot* was written by Wallace (or Wallis) Willis, a slave owned by a Choctaw Indian. While Willis tilled a cotton field at Spencer Academy, a Choctaw Indian boarding school in Oklahoma, the sight of the Red River flowing in the distance reminded him of the Jordan River and the carrying away of the Prophet Elijah in a heavenly chariot. A missionary at the academy, Alexander Reid, heard the hymn and brought it to the East. Some scholars believe this song and *Steal Away,* also composed by Willis, contain hidden references used in assisting slaves to freedom via the Underground Railroad.

CHAPTER 3
BEAR'S PAW

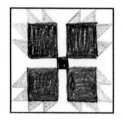

Janine Dunlop – Warren, Michigan

My life began just like it did for most people born in the 1950s. I had a mom and a dad just like everyone else, safe and secure in a "normal" family. My world tipped, however, when my mother delivered a stillborn baby girl, and then went completely off axis when she died a few months later. All this happened before my fourth birthday while my dad battled his demons at the local bar.

After my mother passed, my dad was unable or unwilling to care for me. Quite unlike the jolly song—without passing over a river or through the wood—off to Grandmother's house I went. Grandma, 50 years old when I moved in, felt forced into a situation she never wanted, but with no other choice, she raised her deceased daughter's child.

I never felt I belonged to anyone. My father occasionally dropped in and out of my life, but I was an ever dangling thread, slowly unraveling.

I lived with Grandma until her death. I am thankful she took care of me. She taught me to be the person I am today. Although I am glad circumstances did not force me into the foster system and I was able to stay with a family member, that nagging feeling of not belonging still hung over me.

Soon after Grandma passed, my dad died, too. I was 30 years old. Everyone I was connected with was gone. It was then I knew for certain my thread was at the end of the spool. There was no shoulder to cry on, no one to plan my wedding with, no one to see my children born, and no one for me to talk to or cry with. Life was lonely.

In 1995, something happened that began strengthening the weakened fiber of my life. I saw a new light—a bright, happy light that came from the joy inside a church building. It gleamed from the windows, and I wanted some of that light for myself.

Once inside, the church showered me with love. Peace watered my parched spirit. I was overwhelmed. I had never experienced so much love all at one time or in one place, and this came from complete strangers. I was treated like family, and I just knew God was in this. He brought these people into my life to fill the ache of the ones I had lost. I finally had brothers, sisters, and a Father, and I saw a Scripture fulfilled in my life: "God sets the lonely in families…" (Psalms 68:6, NIV). God did not promise a physical family, although I do have that now with my husband, children, and in-laws. He simply promised a family, and He graciously connected me to a church where I belonged, embraced in love and accepted by its members and by Him.

As I prepared to write about my experiences for this book, I thought of all the calls, cards, hugs, prayers and words of encouragement I have received from people in my church over the years and all the new ways I have grown being a part of this wonderful family. I learned to walk a new way, this time with the Lord. I took baby steps at first, but that is how we all learn, isn't it—one step at a time.

I learned to put my Father first, above all else. That was a hard one. Being alone for so much of my life, my world revolved around taking care of me. After all, I was all I had, so according to my way of thinking, I best look out for my interests. Nobody else was there to do it for me.

I learned to worship with my whole heart and soul without being afraid of what others might think. I feel God's holy presence with me. My spine tingles when Jesus touches me and takes me to a place of total unawareness of anything but Him. Warmth surrounds me that no blanket could provide or no mortal man could give and that Presence seems to follow me, even to work. People see and feel something different about me. They come to me for prayer and tell me I am their "hot line to God." It is wonderful to reach into the lives of others this way and I continue to develop and grow from the deep personal conversations with my spiritual Father, something I always longed for but never experienced with my dad.

Words cannot express the depth of my gratitude—to God for reaching out to me, but also to those special people the Lord used to touch my life. I honor and give thanks to my in laws, but especially my dear mother-in-law, Jessie Dunlop. Because of her, Faith Apostolic Church of Troy became my new family—one that is always here for me, always willing to help in the trials of my life.

I am amazed at how my pastors and other ministers always seem to preach directly to me, knowing my weaknesses and strengths without me ever saying a word. I am grateful for Rev. Mark Reed (deceased) and Rev. Marvin Walker, who have connected with God in ways that have impacted my life and changed me for eternity. I know that while I live on this earth I will always have that longing for my heavenly home, but the yearning to belong has lessened, and I now have a place to go for help. But, first and foremost, I turn to my heavenly Father, for He is all knowing and all powerful, and He knows every thread of my life. Praise God for His marvelous works!

⸎

The Bear's Claw quilt pattern, according to the "Quilt Code," directed runaways to follow an actual trail of a bear's footprints—a sort of road map that indicated the best path for fleeing slaves to take. With most escapes occurring in the spring, when bears awoke from hibernation, it would be easy for a runaway to follow a bear's trail in the moist spring soil, leading them to water and hopefully safety.

The pattern, a Native American motif, may also represent the possible assistance available from the Native Americans who aided runaways as they fled for freedom. Many escaped slaves benefited from their benevolence and eventually settled with the Native American people.

When researching for a quilt pattern that connected to Janine's story, I was immediately impressed with the Bear's Claw. Janine went through a long winter, like a bear in hibernation, but when the season was right, she emerged from her seclusion. Like escaping slaves following the trail of a bear, Janine followed the path God brought her to, the steps of a godly mother-in-law who directed her to the water and provision she needed.

As many of the escaping slaves found refuge among the Native Americans, Janine found solace among the new people God brought into her life, and I am thankful to know her. I never knew her background. I only watched her serve God and others, especially reaching into the lives of children as a devoted Sunday School teacher and demonstrating to the young people in our church honor and respect to their elders by hosting a Senior Saints breakfast twice a year. The class raises the funds, prepares the invitations, decorations, name tags, placemats and food, and then serves those who have given in service to others.

Now I know why she does it. Thank you, Janine. I praise God with you for His marvelous works!

CHAPTER 4
CROSSROADS

Teresa Altman — Trenton, Tennessee

Over the course of several years, Diane and I developed a close friendship. She was one of my coworkers and also the wife of my husband's best friend. Diane and I shared lunches, recipes and evenings together with our husbands. After my divorce, my friendship with Diane cooled rapidly. Phone calls ceased, and our heart-to-heart conversations reduced to brief, muted exchanges in office hallways.

I was a career professional, and now the divorced mother of two toddlers. Prolific rumors circulated around the office about the break-up of my marriage, and every male co-worker assigned to work with me fell victim to unmerciful gossip. I tried to harden myself to the denigration. Outwardly, I wore an aloof demeanor, but in the end, I chose to escape the endless accusations by finding another job. I soon realized that running away or being "unapproachable" would not protect me from the rumors' effect on my character and my family.

One cold winter night, just as I finished bathing and dressing the girls for bed, I heard a knock at my front door. Surprised to have an unexpected visitor at this time, I peeked outside. An unsettling feeling rose when I saw my ex-husband and my parents. We talked and I discovered Diane had reported my rumored transgressions to my ex-husband as though they were facts. Following that revelation, perplexing threats of custody hearings, parenting suitability and spiritual disgrace swarmed in a tangle of intense discussions that lasted throughout the night.

A seed of anger for Diane took root in my heart. For months, it swelled and grew to unimaginable heights, like Jack's bean stalk, stretching into the clouds. Visions of revenge became my central focus and warped my sense of reality. By God's great mercy, all the while I stewed and suffered, He persistently pressed two Bible verses into my heart: "For if you forgive men their trespasses, Your heavenly Father will also forgive you" (Matthew 6:14, NKJV), and "Pray for those who spitefully use you and persecute you" (Matthew 5:44, NKJV).

I knew my anger had disrupted my communion with God. I also knew I was not able to defeat it in my own strength and determination. My heart, heavy and overcome with guilt, pleaded for God to remove the bitterness and forgive my unforgiveness. Although I had no honest compassion for Diane, I knew God's Word instructed me to pray for her. Consistently and obediently, I willed myself to pray that she would receive blessings and salvation from God.

"Father, Your Word tells me that I must forgive before I can be forgiven. But I can't forgive her. I want to please You, Lord, but I am still angry. Please teach me how to forgive her. You said I should pray for my enemies. So until the day You remove my anger and unforgiveness, I will keep praying for her."

The profound sense of betrayal I experienced threatened more than my relationship with my family. It also affected my relationship with God. My daily prayers, rather than seeking relationship with God, became desperate petitions as I prayed for a miraculous erasing of the all-consuming anger that threatened my relationship with Him.

Then one day the inevitable came. While grocery shopping, I sent my eight-year-old daughter to an adjacent aisle for cereal. She returned with company. "Mama, this is Jenny, my new friend at school," she announced.

"Hi!" Jenny exuberantly added. "My mom says she used to work with you. Her name is Diane, and she's in the next aisle."

Oh, no! For six years I had obediently prayed, but still did not feel ready to truly forgive Diane. Silently I prayed, pleading with God. "Father, please let this moment pass from me. I am not ready!" At that very moment, Diane pushed her loaded buggy around the corner and walked down the aisle toward me. Then she stopped.

As I looked at her, I saw something different than I expected. I did not recognize this woman as the same one who shattered my life six years earlier. Neither did I see the woman who had once been my friend. Instead, I saw a lost and lonely child afraid of what she was facing as she met me in the aisle. An unexpected compassion overwhelmed me, and I immediately realized God had answered my prayers. He faithfully provided the miracle I asked for, and the scene changed with such speed I cannot recall closing the distance between us. My next memory was just holding Diane in my arms and saying, "I love you, Diane." And I meant it.

I thank God for setting me free from the anger that consumed me for so many years and allowing me to see my old friend through His eyes of love.

According to the "Quilt Code," the Crossroads quilt pattern represented a city of refuge for escaping slaves. The main crossroad, or Underground Railroad terminal, was the city of Cleveland, Ohio. Several overland trails connected with Cleveland, and from there many water passages led across Lake Erie into Canada and freedom.

Traditional Crossroads quilt patterns look like an X with an off-color square center. Examining the pattern, you might wonder why the box in the middle is a different color, breaking up the flow of the X, but I find the design parallels with Teresa's story. Unforgiveness blocks our way: our way to others, and our way to God.

When Teresa encountered Diane at the grocery, she reached a crossroads in the store aisle—and in her life. She wisely chose to turn from the hurt and betrayal she felt and turn instead to God for the grace and strength to extend forgiveness to Diane.

Forgiveness is a choice, a choice that frees the forgiver. When we face the decision to release or harbor unforgiveness, we confront our own crossroads. May we have the humility and courage to respond with the same grace Teresa offered at her crossroads experience.

Quilting, a necessary task that evolved into a high art form, finds its roots in poverty and need. In antebellum America, the well-to-do did not salvage scraps from discarded clothing to make blankets, but those in need used every resource at their disposal. A scrap quilt made by an enslaved woman in a darkened plantation cabin long ago would be of great value today. Similarly, the lessons we learn in our own dark cabins, in our own times of difficulty and need—those lessons are often of the highest value in our lives.

CHAPTER 5
LOG CABIN

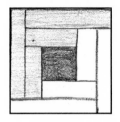

Susan Paurazas — Rochester Hills, Michigan

It was the perfect lazy summer Sunday afternoon. Black-eyed Susans and daisies were in full bloom and the fresh cut grass was warm under bare feet. My daughter Ann and her friend Carrie were playing in the back yard, picking daisies and dandelions scattered over the lawn like dots of butter.

The girls collected enough flowers to make bouquets for their mothers, then climbed in the tree house—an escape from the hot sun and Carrie's younger sister. "She can be such a pest," said Carrie. "I'm glad she's taking a nap now. I just want to play—not baby-sit."

Carrie looked intently at Ann. "I tried calling you all morning. Where were you?"

"It's Sunday, Carrie. We were at church and then we went out for breakfast."

"Oh. I forgot."

"What church do you go to?" asked Ann. "I've never seen you at mine."

"We don't go to church," said Carrie matter-of-factly. "That's why you've never seen me there, and that's probably why I forgot it was Sunday."

"Why don't you go to church?"

"My mom and dad can't take us."

"Why not?"

"Because my mom likes to sleep in late," Carrie explained. "She says she needs to catch up on her sleep and Sundays are the only days she can do that."

"Well, you could always go to a later service," Ann suggested.

"My dad has to do the yard work." Carrie shrugged her slight shoulders. "Since he works during the week, the weekend is the only time he says he can get his chores done. So my mom and dad are both busy on Sunday."

"Oh…" Ann paused and tried to think of a solution. "I guess you can still say prayers at home."

"Yeah, I guess so, but we don't do that. Sometimes we say grace before dinner, like at special occasions like Thanksgiving and Christmas, but that's about the only time we pray."

Ann sat in the tree house thinking about what Carrie had said, absent-mindedly plucking daisy petals. "He loves me," she tugged a moist petal and dropped it to the floor of the tree house. "He loves me not."

"Who loves you?" asked Carrie. "Are you thinking of you-know-who from school?"

"No! I was not thinking of anybody," replied Ann defensively, knowing that even if she had been, she was not going to tell Carrie. Carrie was not good at keeping secrets.

"Tell me!' insisted Carrie.

"There's nothing to tell, really."

"Carrie!" her mom yelled across the lawn. "Time for lunch!"

"I gotta go," said Carrie.

"Don't forget your mom's flowers."

"Thanks."

The girls scrambled out of the tree house. Ann watched Carrie disappear inside her home, and then walked in the house with a thoughtful look on her face.

"Thank you, Ann," I said, taking the bouquet of yellow flowers she offered. "They're beautiful."

I pulled a vase from the cabinet to put the flowers in water. "I see some of the daisies have petals missing."

"I was playing He loves me—He loves me not."

"What did you end on?"

"He loves me."

"Oh, good. Whoever 'he' is, I'm glad he loves you," I teased.

"Mom, there's really not anyone I'm thinking of."

"Okay," I said, "but I know of somebody who loves you. For example, there's me, Daddy, your sister, and God, of course."

"Thanks, Mom." Ann's lips curved upwards in a sweet smile.

I watched the wheels spin as Ann replayed her conversation with Carrie and then shared it with me. "Carrie doesn't talk to God," Ann said, her concern evident.

"Sounds like they just don't want to go to church," I said.

"But how will God know about Carrie if she doesn't talk to Him?" Ann asked, bewildered.

It was one of those times a child's question throws you off balance and leaves you searching for answers. I took a deep breath, thought hard for a minute, and attempted to formulate an answer that made sense to both of us.

"Well," I began, "God is everywhere, Ann. He knows all of us, even if we don't talk to Him regularly. God is very patient. He will wait for us." I paused and looked at Ann. She was listening intently. "It's like God is waiting, looking out the window, expecting someone to come home, and when He sees them, He jumps up to greet them. God is always happy to see them."

"He'll probably have to wait a long time for Carrie and her family," Ann said. "He'll probably get tired of waiting."

"Not really. God has lots of other people to talk to, but He doesn't forget about the people who don't talk to Him. He keeps hoping and waiting to hear from them, and when they pray and talk to Him, it makes Him very happy. God especially likes to hear from children. He listens to children. They are very special to Him."

I looked at my daughter. She was thinking on what I said, pondering the meaning. I hoped my answer was satisfactory. We were silent for a minute, and then she spoke with resolve. "Let's make sure He remembers us, Mom. Let's say a prayer right now just to let God know we didn't forget Him."

"Good idea," I said. "A prayer doesn't always mean we're asking for something. A prayer can just mean we're checking in with God, letting Him know we're thinking of Him and are glad He's always there for us."

We folded our hands. "Dear God," Ann began, "We just wanted to say hi and thank you for everything. We are doing fine and we hope You are, too. I hope You get to talk to Carrie soon. She's nice and I think it would be good for her to talk to You, even if she can't go to church. Amen."

"That was a very nice prayer, Ann. I think God liked it."

"I think so, too," she said. "I hope Carrie talks to Him. God always likes to make a new friend."

"And you never have to worry about He loves me not," I added with a smile as I plucked off the last daisy petal.

~~~

The Log Cabin quilt block may have indicated a safe house for escaping slaves, perhaps one particular log cabin in Cleveland. Another possibility was a signal to weather out the winter before traveling on or perhaps establish permanent residence in a "free" area.

Traditionally, the center block of a Log Cabin quilt is red, representing the center of the home, the hearth or fire. A variance to the traditional pattern, a black center block, was said to indicate a safe house, while a yellow center meant to look for a light for a place to enter for provision and shelter.

Yet another possible meaning turns the tables on the messaging system. Ozella suggested the signal transmitted a message from slave to free, drawing a log cabin in the dirt on the shores of the Great Lakes signaled boat captains that runaway slaves were nearby looking for transportation to Canada.

In every house, every "cabin," there is a center, a hub. To those blessed to be in a Christian environment, our faith in God lights our homes. As we build relationships with those around us, we notice the warm light of God's love is not always present in the lives of others.

Susan's story, her daughter's story really, prompted me to consider my neighbors more carefully and appreciate the relationship we as believers are privileged to have with God. The freedom faith offers is something to treasure and share in love, with our families and those we meet. May our homes be centers of safety, provision and shelter for all who enter.

And just a bit of follow-up, Susan and her daughter did invite Carrie to church. Although she never joined the Paurazas family in worship, her family now attends services at another local congregation.

Juneteenth, also known as Freedom Day or Emancipation Day, originated in Galveston, Texas, in 1865. The day commemorates the ending of slavery in Texas, but is now celebrated worldwide. Though the Emancipation Proclamation was issued on September 22, 1862, it was not enforced in Texas until June 19, 1865. Union General George Granger and 2,000 federal troops arrived in Galveston and enforced the emancipation of its slaves.

CHAPTER 6
SHOOFLY

Kimberly Sciscoe – Dallas, Texas

The guard rang the bell that released the series of gates and doors. "Be careful, young lady. There are a lot of crazy people in there!" The doors clanged shut behind me, and I entered a foreign world eerily absent of color and warmth. Disease, desperation and death hung like black clouds, and the stench made me long for the fresh air I had just left behind.

Unsmiling people roamed the hallways. Profanities rose above the raging music, and guards broke up fights repeatedly. "So this is the hidden side to the world of drugs and alcohol," I thought to myself. "The side you never see on the billboards."

A bell rang and the narrow hallway flooded with yelling, fighting people. I tried to disappear in the crowd, but my innocence, a red flag waving, drew looks and taunts that terrified me. Frantic, I searched for an exit. I had to get out.

Then I remembered my promise to Dave and Ron. Ex-druggies and alcoholics, Dave and Ron had been teaching Bible studies to convicts and homeless people at this rehabilitation center. They asked me to join them in hopes of attracting women to the Bible study. I could not let them down.

Praying under my breath, I searched until I found Dave and Ron in the meeting room. As I was about to enter, a young woman passed in the hallway. I followed her and worked up the courage to speak. "Hi. I'm Kimberly. What's your name?"

"Mary," she snapped. I looked into her hollow eyes and invited her to the Bible study. "I'll see," she said as she walked off.

Ten minutes later Mary walked through the door. I smiled and motioned for her to sit next to me. She listened to Dave's and Ron's testimonies of deliverance wearing the same disappointment and hopelessness as the others.

Watching Mary, a deep compassion gripped my heart. I wanted to reach out to her, but I did not know where to start. We spoke after the Bible study, and when I asked, she said, "I've tried to read the Bible before, but I don't really understand it."

Before I knew it, I asked Mary if she would like me to come early next week so we could study the Bible together. "Why would you want to come back here?" she asked, eyeing me suspiciously. Her question stunned me, but 19 years of living in the streets had taught Mary that everyone had a motive.

I felt God's Spirit rise up inside me. "Mary, I want to come back because you are worth it," I said. "Jesus died for you and He hasn't given up on you. He has the answers you are searching for, and I want to help you find them." Mary looked at me in disbelief, but a twinge of hope lit in her eyes.

As I left the cheerless building and thought about the wretched souls inside, my 25 years began playing in reverse. Like a motion picture, I saw my parents loving and nurturing me, raising me with godly principles and modeling the love of Jesus time and again. Positive encounters with schoolteachers replayed in my mind. Recollections of thousands of church services and the many times I received love and encouragement from pastors and youth workers—memories of Bible camps and conferences where I had been saturated by the presence of God. I felt gluttonous.

A tidal wave of conviction flooded my spirit. I asked God to forgive me for the years I spent receiving without giving, choosing to focus on my comfortable world and closing my eyes to the pain of others. That day I realized my Christian upbringing and training had all been for this day—the day my eyes were opened to see beyond myself to a lost world.

Tuesday finally came. Back at the center, I learned that Mary had come from an affluent family and gotten involved with the wrong crowd in high school. Experimenting with marijuana, she turned to harder drugs, and addictions eventually forced her into the streets. She stole to survive, sleeping wherever she found shelter.

Mary knew if she failed to stay clean after this third time at the rehab center, she would go to jail. "If you truly surrender to God," I told her, "He will help you break the cycle and you can live a drug-free life."

We explored Scriptures, and I invited Mary to come to church with me. I worked all week to convince the rehab center's director to let her go. She was embarrassed about her dirty clothes, so I brought her something to wear and Sunday morning we drove to church.

Mary enjoyed the Sprit of God moving freely in the service and I got her back on time, creating goodwill with the guards. Over the next weeks, Mary and I shared more Bible studies and trips to church, even an outing to my home for dinner. Little by little, she began to trust me. With this trust, she also began opening her heart to the Word of God and saw areas in her life that needed change.

I will never forget the Saturday night of Mary's baptism and the Sunday morning she received the glorious gift of the Holy Ghost. From that day until this, neither Mary nor I have ever been the same.

I did not have to live a day in Mary's shoes to minister to her. God had already delivered thousands of drug addicts and He knew just what Mary needed to hear. He simply chose me to be the vessel through which He spoke, and He did all the rest.

In the rehab center, I felt God's presence more strongly than in any church service or Bible camp meeting. When I looked around the center, instead of seeing addicts, I saw people ready to receive God's answers of love and hope. A certain peace settled in the room as we read about Jesus coming to earth to seek and save the lost.

My faith in God's transforming power dwarfed my fears. Week after week, darkness gave way to more light. As Mary experienced freedom in her life, I realized a liberation of my own, unintimidated by the pasts of others and free from the fear that I would be unable to relate to people like Mary.

During the summer, many from the center came to church. I was absolutely thrilled as I watched them lift their hands in worship and their faces light up in the presence of God. In just a few months, the lives of 15 people were transformed by the power of God.

Soul winning became my new hobby. I was hooked. I could feel God calling me to be an everyday witness, maybe even one of those radical soul winners. It felt better than gardening; better than redecorating my house; even better than shopping at an outlet mall for 75 percent off!

Fear had lost its hold on me. I was finally free.

⁓⌒⌒⌒

The Shoofly quilt pattern, according to Ozella' telling of the "Quilt Code," is said to represent an actual person who helped escaping slaves. This person, possibly a free black, secretly aided fugitives, hiding them in churches and caves. Often on the outskirts of towns or close to rivers, "Shoofly" frequently utilized graveyards as hiding places, as well. Ozella indicated the Shoofly block served as a signal for runaways to "scatter, so you won't be caught."

One source identified Shoofly as a possible nickname for Harriett Tubman. A runaway turned conductor on the Underground Railroad, Mrs. Tubman assisted some three hundred slaves to freedom over a period of ten years. If Mrs. Tubman was indeed "Shoofly," the song Shoo Fly, Don't Bother Me, would take on a new meaning, as well.

Shoofly Sciscoe—that's going to be my new nickname for Kimberly. Containing twofold lessons, Kimberly's story first inspires me to look beyond my own fears and perceived shortcomings and reach out to others with the healing power of God's love. I have heard someone say, "Do it scared," and I think that is a lesson we can all learn. As we step out in faith and "do it scared," we can experience the same type of liberty and freedom Kimberly received.

Secondly, beyond the opportunity of liberty from our personal fears, like Kimberly, we can become "shooflies" aiding others on their journeys to freedom, and we, too, can "feel like a morning star."

Shoo, fly, don't bother me,
Shoo, fly, don't bother me,
Shoo, fly, don't bother me,
For I belong to somebody.

I feel, I feel,
I feel like a morning star,
I feel, I feel,
I feel like a morning star.

Moses: Harriet Tubman, nicknamed the "Moses" of her people, professed there were two things she had a right to, liberty or death. "If I could not have one," she said, "I would have the other." The night Harriet ran away from her master in Maryland, she sang a coded song of farewell. "I'll Meet You In The Morning, I'm Bound For The Promised Land," sent a message to her mother of her planned escape. Once free, Harriet voluntarily returned to the land of her captivity 19 times. Over the course of ten years and at great personal risk, she served as the most famous conductor on the Underground Railroad, and in her own words, "I nebber run my train off de track." During the Civil War, Harriet served as a cook, a nurse and a spy for federal forces in South Carolina and she became the first woman to lead an armed assault. Tubman was tenacious, with a Rosa Parks spirit, refusing to move to the smoking car of a New York train, her arm broken as she clutched the railing. Among Tubman's remarkable experiences, a doctor operated on her head, lifting her skull, without anesthesia. She chose to bite a bullet as she had seen Civil War soldiers do during amputations.

Chapter 7
Bowtie

Cynthia Khan – Troy, Michigan

I was born in Lahore, Pakistan, in 1956. My grandmother, a Hindu, came to Christ through missionaries who brought the Christian message to the people of India. A predominantly Hindu society, India is also home to Muslims and Sikhs and, thanks to the efforts of missionaries, some Christians.

A tomboy growing up in Pakistan, I spent my days playing boys' games with my two brothers. We cycled, climbed trees, flew kites, and played marbles in the street. Life was simple, but we had so much fun. Our close-knit families were rich in love and respect for parents and teachers and we had a strong sense of belonging.

My mother, an educationist, was the principal and owner of a private English school in Lahore. A strong Christian woman, Mother was widowed when I was 14. She never remarried, but dedicated her life to serving the Lord by serving others. Her motto, "live for others," was witnessed by her children and our entire neighborhood, an example of commitment and sacrifice.

I attended Kinnaird College for Women, a prestigious women's college. Since my father's death, Mother had prayed for my husband. In the East in the 1970s, marriages were arranged by the families. Mother prayed and asked God to choose my husband. When I was 20 years old, someone asked for my hand. Mother was certain this request was God's will. She liked everything she saw: the groom, the family and their strong Christian faith.

I married at 22 and lived with my in-laws in the village of Shanitnagar. My husband's grandfather, raised Muslim, had come to the Lord through missionaries who traveled to India when it was under British rule. God used him to establish the first Christian village in the area, but in 1997, a mob of 3,000 Muslims devastated it. Putting it to fire, they destroyed houses and ripe crops and took away the young girls.

The attack was the result of a false accusation of blasphemy. In Pakistan people live under the Shariah or Islamic Law. According to this blasphemy law, if any Christian says anything against Islam or its prophet, Mohammad, they receive a death sentence without any court hearing or explanation.

In March 1979, in pursuit of a better future, my husband left for Saudi Arabia. Four years passed before I was able to join him, during which I saw him once every eight to ten months. In 1983, our 2 children and I finally joined him in Al Khobar. There we witnessed U.S. troops marching the streets during Desert Storm.

Life was very different in Saudi Arabia. Women were not allowed to drive, so I stayed home. When my husband arrived in the evenings, we would go shopping or for a drive. We were on the street one day when a Mutawa (religious police) stopped us. He had a stick in his hand, and he told my husband I needed to wear the abaya (an Islamic garb that covers from head to toe and a head scarf), otherwise, he would be jailed. We were so scared we went straight to the store and bought the covering and for the ten years we lived in Saudi Arabia, I never took it off.

People from all over the world worked in Saudi Arabia, but only Muslims were allowed to practice their faith. If a foreigner brought in non-Islamic religious material, they were arrested at the airport, jailed and tortured. Everything was censored.

After living under the strict laws for some time, my husband and I strongly felt the need to meet with fellow Christians. There are no organized churches in Saudi Arabia, but expatriates had special permission from the king to conduct worship service in the gym of the Arab American Oil Company Compound. Only residents of the compound were allowed to attend the service, but through an American colleague from my husband's work, at the risk of our lives and the lives of the people who took us, we were able to pass through tight security and participate in services. In these services, I experienced a strong and vibrant church. People completely engrossed in worship unified with a visible hunger for God's Word that erased denominational differences.

It was there my husband and I felt a call to full-time ministry, and we prayed for God to show us the way. Our American friend was instrumental in seeing this accomplished. He provided material from the Lutheran Church that started us on our journey. We applied for immigration to Canada. Five months later, with our four children and all we owned, we landed in Toronto and became members of St. Marks Lutheran Church.

One Sunday a missionary from Detroit delivered a message that changed our lives. He told us about POBLO, People of the Book Lutheran Outreach, and a missionary society founded by Dearborn circuit pastors with a passion to reach Muslims, a large community of which lived in Dearborn. The name, POBLO, was taken from the Quran, the Muslim holy book, in which "people of the book" are identified as Jews and Christians who had the "book" (message) before Muslims. This seemed an appropriate name for a mission society reaching out to Muslims.

My husband and I were the first Asian Missionaries to join POBLO. Since we had newly moved to Canada, we could not just pack up and leave the country. We lived there five years, commuting from Windsor to Michigan, before we were able to apply for permanent immigrant status in the States.

We went through all this because God uses ordinary people to take the Word to the world. It is exciting to see churches planted in different cultures and languages and reach people from different backgrounds. Although it was a difficult journey, transitioning from Pakistan to Saudi Arabia to Canada to Michigan, it is wonderful to live in this land that offers freedom to all—freedom of religion and freedom of speech.

I say to my brothers and sisters born in this great country, "You are blessed and privileged. Your forefathers sacrificed to establish a system that has proven to be the best." The Constitution, based on Christian values, allows people from every tongue, tribe, race, or faith to enjoy equal rights. I wish people living in this country valued what they have. In the countries where I lived, strict Islamic law was enforced. Even non-Muslims lived according to Muslim law. No one was exempt. No one could raise a voice against the system or the government.

I thank God for bringing my family to this land where we not only worship and praise God freely and openly, but we are also able to take the Word to those who have not heard it. God bless America and all those who live in this free land.

⌒⌒⌒

A Bow Tie quilt pattern was said to be a directive for fleeing slaves to dress in conventional attire, to blend in with the people in the community. A suggested symbol to disguise or change clothing to a person of higher status, a Bow Tie quilt on display purportedly signaled runaways to stay in hiding until fresh apparel could be brought to them–clothes that obscured their status and permitted them to travel undetected to ships and other passages that would take them on their way to Canada and freedom.

Cynthia's story, in part that of a Christian disguised by a Muslim veil, easily relates to the Bow Tie pattern. Necessary for survival, her forced masquerade kept Cynthia safe until she was able to leave a nation hostile to Christians and live in a land of freedom.

Regardless of our race, language or homeland, I believe every person hungers for a relationship with God, and it is beautiful to see God use the hardships Cynthia and her family endured as stepping stones to ministry. She now freely lives out her faith and shares her faith with others.

In addition to the message of salvation through Jesus alone, Cynthia's clarion call sounds an appeal to the blessed citizens of America—to appreciate the liberty they have and exercise with joy the freedom to worship God according to individual beliefs. Yes, Cynthia, may God bless America, and coast-to-coast, border-to-border, in the hearts of men, women and children throughout the great land, let freedom ring.

CHAPTER 8
DOUBLE WEDDING RINGS

Susan Snover – Hazel Park, Michigan

I was a quiet, shy little girl afraid of my own shadow. Insecurity fueled my doubts of any personal worth, and an abiding fear, often of what others thought of me, contributed to feelings of being unloved and unlovable.

As a young girl, unmentionable traumatic experiences changed my life and I burrowed deeply in a cocoon of timid reserve and fear. Unsure who I could talk to, I wondered if I should talk at all. I kept my feelings to myself, certain I would be hated or turned away if I shared them. Insecurity demanded I not make trouble for anyone else.

When I became a teen, I decided to stand up and take control of my life. I wanted to be loved, and I wanted that love to be on my terms for a change. Clueless as to how my "take-charge" choices would affect my life, the decisions I made to fix things soon spun them more out of control than ever.

Pregnant at fifteen, the baby's father and I married, but sorrow multiplied when one month before my sixteenth birthday, I gave birth to a stillborn baby boy. The loss was so painful. I fell into a deep depression. In nightmares and throughout the day I had visions of my baby blaming me for his death. In that dream-world way, the baby could talk, and he cried out over and over, "I hate you for letting me die!"

At night I would lay in bed pounding my stomach until my husband wrestled me back to reality. Over time, probably due in large part to my inability to deal with the death of our baby, my husband left me. Divorced at seventeen, my depression spiraled into thoughts of suicide. Counseling helped and with my mother's encouragement, I reenrolled and threw myself into my schoolwork and graduated on time with my class.

After graduation, I met and married a sweet man. We had three beautiful children, two boys and a girl. Throughout the ten years of our marriage I continued to struggle with my emotions and insecurities. Over time, our relationship disintegrated until it finally broke completely. This time I filed for divorce.

On my own for about a year and a half, I lived a bit on the wild side, not really caring about anything except my children. My first husband and I remarried, but things were different between us. I no longer allowed anyone to "boss" me and was not the sweet, kind girl he knew at sixteen. My husband had changed, too. He did not talk as much any more, and his interests differed from when we were first married. Although he liked the wild-and-crazy Sue, he missed the sweet-and-innocent girl he had known before.

Disregarding my doctor's advice, I conceived again. This time my husband and I had a beautiful, healthy boy. We were happy, but as time passed, we seemed to pull away from each other and separated many times.

During one of our separations, I took off up north. I took my youngest son and left with another man. We stayed at his father's house while our trailer was supposedly getting ready for us to move into. Basically a farm maid in my new fling's father's house, I cared for his infant brother and the animals, made the meals and taxied people about. To my surprise, the man I was with was arrested. While he was in jail, his father offered to have my husband killed. This really got my attention. Frightened, I told him I could never have my son's father killed, even if we weren't getting along. My eyes were opened, and I realized I still cared for my husband, even though I was with another man.

I knew my life was a mess, and when Sunday came around, I decided to visit a church I had seen in town. Alone and scared, I thought I would be safe in church, and I was, except from myself and God. When I arrived on Sunday morning, I was placed in a class, and the topic of the day?...love, marriage, family, and sticking things out through the hard times.

The lesson hit hard, but I visited again the following week. It was more of the same. According to the Bible, divorce was not an option.

When I first moved north, my daughter planned to follow, moving up after I got settled. She called to tell me she decided not to move, but she still wanted to come for a visit. After we hung up I cried in my room for hours, but I came to a resolution. When my daughter's visit ended, I would pack up and go home too. And I did.

Unable to get everything in one trip, my husband returned with me to retrieve the rest of my things. We had no plans to stay together as husband and wife, but I soon discovered that God's plans, though sometimes unexpected and painful, are always for the best.

While we retrieved the rest of my belongings, I broke my foot and was unable to work or get a place of my own. Instead I was forced to rely on my husband to take care of me. Grounded and dependant, I began talking to him again. We decided to leave the past behind and try to work things out.

A year passed and things were still rocky. In a financial mess, I attempted to raise money to save our home working for a financial services company. On a reluctant referral from a friend, the family I met offered me a ticket to an Easter presentation at their church. I accepted it and said I would go, without a clue that my life was about to change in a dramatic way.

When I walked in the church I felt for the first time the love my soul had longed for. It captured my heart, like a moth to the flame, and I was hooked. Over time, the love of Jesus stabilized my emotions and continues to help me work through the insecurities that plagued me through so much of my life. The presence of God brings healing to the deep wounds of the past, and I am free from the desperate searching that consumed my thoughts. I know God is not finished with me yet, but I have finally found my worth. It is not found in me, but who I am in God.

In church for four years now, my husband and I are still together. My children are often in church beside me and I thank God for leading me home, even though I had no idea where home was. Life is still no bed of roses, but God in my life makes living a whole lot better.

Interlocking rings, the motif of the Double Wedding Rings quilt pattern, dates back to Fourth Century Roman cups. To make the unique design, scraps of every color and hue are stitched into blocks that, when standing alone, look like four-petal flowers on a solid background. When grouped together, they create a beautiful work of linked rings.

The "Quilt Code" instructed fleeing slaves to "dress up in cotton and satin bow ties and go to the cathedral church, get married, and exchange double wedding rings." Ring exchanges were not the common practice in wedding ceremonies in antebellum society. Ozella proposed the pattern meant that slave rings could be cut off in the safety of churches, the stained-glass windows hiding the activity taking place inside. It may also have meant, in conjunction with the Bow Ties pattern, that slaves should appear to be free by their outward appearance. Not only would a change in clothing help them blend into society, but also wearing a wedding ring. Slaves, barred from legal marriages, would not have worn a ring, and the item would give an additional outward appearance of freedom.

When I think of a double wedding, I think of two couples getting married at the same time. In Susan's case, before she became a follower of Jesus, her "double wedding" occurred when she wed the same man twice. Like the interlocking rings of the Double Wedding Ring quilt pattern, Susan's story illustrates how the pieces of a life, before and after a born-again experience, connect to make one complete design. The individual blocks make one image, but when brought together, an entirely different pattern emerges—a visually interesting and lovely one.

The way the arcs of the pattern connect to make interlocking circles reminds me of how so many of life's aspects overlap. Susan's struggles with self-esteem and insecurity did not "stand alone"—each in its own little compartment. Instead, they spiraled into the other pieces. Now God's love is doing the same thing, one ring at a time, working its way through the pieces of her days, her emotions, and her experiences.

Susan retains a bit of girlhood shyness, but with it she now wears a radiant smile, yet another connection to the Double Wedding Rings pattern. The many arcs used to make the design look like smiles pieced together to create a cheery quilt top.

How the Underground Railroad got its name: The Underground Railroad was a complex network of routes that assisted runaway slaves to freedom. A variety of groups utilized its hundreds of paths that stretched through many states. Conductors, often former slaves, helped the "passengers," hiding them, providing food and giving them directions to the next safe house. A railroad with no tracks, the Underground Railroad, according to a tale told in the South, received its name from a man chasing a runaway slave.

In 1831, as Tice Davids tried to escape from Kentucky to Ohio, his master trailed not far behind. Davids plunged into the Ohio and swam across the river towards Ripley. His master kept a keen eye on him, even as he located a boat and crossed the river after him. Davids swam safely to shore and disappeared in an instant. His master was never able to find him and he reasoned Davids "must of gone off on an underground railroad." See Chapter 16 for more information on the Underground Railroad in Ripley, Ohio.

CHAPTER 9
FLYING GEESE

Pam English – Chesterfield, Michigan

As we pass through the days of our lives, we do not always recognize the hand of God at work, but in reflection, His handiwork becomes obvious. When I look back, I can see the Lord actively worked on my behalf, even when I did not realize it.

Of little financial means, my husband Ron and I were married 16 years without ever owning our own home. In 1998, we walked through a house a friend was living in, knowing it would be coming up for sale. I absolutely loved it. I felt the Lord impress me saying, "This is your house," but when I shared this with my husband, he just rolled his eyes and said, "Yeah."

Nine months later I gave birth to my dream when we signed on the dotted line and my husband and I became owners of the very home God had told me was mine. I cherished the house, because I knew it had come from the Lord.

We enjoyed our home for many years as we watched our children grow from teens into young adults. We had come into the church when William was 6 and Mary was 4. Like every parent, we hoped and prayed our children, now 22 and 20, had adopted for themselves the Christian principles we held dear.

In December 2006, Mary and I had an argument regarding the friends she was running with and she left our home on foot. I so badly wanted to run after her and bring her back home, but the "tough love mother" in me said, "Let her see what it is like in the big world on her own." This was very hard for me, but Mary came by her stubborn streak honestly. She got it from her mom, and I knew that if I played to her game, I would be like Silly Putty in her hands. That couldn't happen.

Mary chose to live in a place she knew I would not approve of and once again, I had to muster up more "tough love" and bite my tongue. We did not talk for several painful weeks, but after a time, we started talking again. Weeks and then months passed. It broke my heart when I realized that no matter how hard I talked or encouraged her to come home, her mind was made up. I told Mary that although I did not approve of her living situation, I loved her and she was always welcome to come home.

In March 2006, Mary told us she was pregnant. Unmarried and pregnant is tough for a mom to handle, but I came to a point where I realized I had done the best I could and had to accept the realities of the situation we now faced. I loved the idea of being a grandma, even if the situation wasn't the best. It certainly was not the baby's fault his mom and dad were not married.

One evening, in celebration of our 23rd anniversary, Ron and I made plans for a dinner date. Our plans were curtailed by mechanical problems with Ron's truck. He attempted to fix it himself, to no avail, which made him angry on top of angry.

Ron has suffered a lot of loss in his life. His father died when he was young. His mother and grandmother passed later in life and a rift with his sister caused him to lose another important relationship for many years. Up to this point, Ron had never fully dealt with the anger he carried from so many losses. Dealing with his truck, our plans falling through, the situation with Mary—it all sandbagged on him and he felt he just could not deal with anything more. With his anger roiling and growing, Ron plunged into depression and threatened suicide twice that day. What a way to spend a wedding anniversary.

I had no idea what was in store for me from there. Things were going to get a lot tougher before this trial was over. On May 26, Ron quit his job leaving us with only my steady paycheck, but without health insurance. Seven weeks passed before Ron found a part-time job at a grocery store. By this time, he had seen a doctor and begun taking anti-depressants. His mood swings seemed somewhat stabilized. In those seven weeks, I continued working, but my paycheck alone could not make the mortgage payments. We were already one month behind and it was not long before a foreclosure notice arrived. I was heart-broken. On September 12, our house was sold at a sheriff's sale to the highest bidder. It seemed like such a loss.

Throughout the previous two years, every couple of months the same nightmare replayed in my sleep. Startled, my heart raced, and for the moments before I realized I was waking from a bad dream, I would say, "You're in the wrong bed. You're in the wrong house. How did you get here? If the owners come home, you will be in trouble." I never understood what the dreams meant. I just knew they troubled me and I had a hard time going back to sleep after them.

In August of 2006, we moved into an apartment, our precious grandson was born on October 29, and our daughter married the father of her baby in January 2007. I would not trade one thing for this precious grandson. He is an absolute joy. My husband has been employed by a great company for about six months. He likes his job and his depression has subsided. Since moving from our home, I have not had any more nightmares, and looking back, I believe the Lord was preparing me through my dreams, telling me He had a different place for me to lay my head.

I still struggled with sorrow about losing my house. Counsel from a friend from church, Carolyn McKenzie, helped me come to terms with everything. "The Lord sometimes gives us things 'for a season,' and your season in that house was probably just over," she said. "Leave it in the hands of the Lord."

I accepted her advice, and let me tell you, the Lord gave me such a peace when I came to terms with the path I was on. From that day forward I knew the Lord was steering the ship of my life. I've learned that when I face trials with patience and a positive outlook, I can learn life's lessons and have peace. God has the map for our paths.

❧⁂❧

The Flying Geese pattern, according to Ozella's "Quilt Code" instructed slaves to follow the lead of migrating geese. Timing their flights to freedom by nature's cues, the best time for slaves to escape coincided with the season geese fly north—Spring. Honking noises and flight paths overhead marked the way to Canada and guided refugees to waterways.

The Flying Geese pattern is one of the oldest and simplest piecework designs, traditionally made in stripes. Three triangles—one "goose" and two "sky"—create a half block. Geese fly in long straight lines from one edge of the quilt to the other, usually alternating with stripes of solid colors. A common variation of the design breaks up the long lines and uses four smaller units or lines of geese. Rows of two or three "geese" fly in the four directions of the compass to create this interesting variance to the original pattern.

Reportedly, abolitionists along the Underground Railroad used Flying Geese quilts to direct escaping slaves. A Flying Geese quilt created a large, graphic arrow that could be displayed to mark a path to freedom.

Seasons change. Birds fly south, then north, then south again. Seasonal changes occur in our lives as well. As I read Pam's story, I thought about the freedom she found when she trusted God to guide her path. We have all been there, haven't we? Facing situations where we attempt to keep control or at least understand, we sympathize with Pam's struggle to hold on—to keep something she felt God had given her. But in doing so, Pam forfeited her peace, and so will we.

When Pam surrendered her hopes and dreams into God's hands, she experienced a peace that comes only from Him—the Bible says in Philippians 4:7 a peace "beyond understanding." That is the best kind of "peace-work" to wrap up in on a cold dark night.

Freedom comes when we learn that the Lord is truly the light that shines on the pavers of our days. Sometimes it would be nice to hear an obnoxious honking when we are looking for the way to take. But like the direction provided in the Flying Geese quilt pattern, God guides our steps on the path of our lives, one day and decision at a time, revealing the way from this land of limitations to the freedom that waits for us in our eternal home.

Flying Geese quilts can help us keep a healthy perspective on life: for every triangle of goose, there are two triangles of sky. When you look at a completed work, there are many little geese, but one immense sky. We serve a big God, and He knows right where we are. Don't forget to look up!

Tragic Attempts: Margaret Garner was born a slave in Boone County, Kentucky. At 15 she married Robert Garner and they had one son. Her husband was often sent away to work leaving Margaret for long periods of time. Margaret gave birth to three light-skinned children, each born a few months after the plantation owner's own children. On January 28, 1856, Margaret, Robert and their children made a daring escape, fleeing across the frozen Ohio River to Cincinatti.

Slave catchers found the Garners barricaded in a house. As the posse stormed the house, Margaret killed her two-year-old-daughter with a butcher knife rather than see her returned to a life of slavery. She was intent on killing all her children, but was subdued and captured. Traveling home on a steamboat, Margaret and her nine-month-old baby Priscilla were thrown overboard when the boat began to sink. Margaret reported that she was happy her baby had died and that she tried to drown herself.

C HAPTER 10
DRUNKARD'S PATH

Terry Michaels — San Marcos, Texas

The second time I got drunk, I was with Jimmy. I am pretty sure it was his first. My first time was quite by accident. It began with the girl next door daring me to eat chili peppers. After frying my gullet with nature's wicked spices, she poured nasty chasers from her parents' liquor cabinet and challenged me to chug the stuff down. The unidentified liquids tasted like kerosene as they ate their way down my tender throat. But as any brave, twelve-year-old would do, I took it like a man and woke up on my front lawn hours later.

My first time drunk also led to my first hangover. I remember staring at my green reflection in toilet water as I spouted off like a seasick beluga. I never wanted to drink again after that, but Jimmy convinced me otherwise.

Standing anxiously in front of the shady liquor store waiting for the perfect stranger to arrive, we kept our eyes out for anyone with that tell-tale look—non-threatening, compliant and sympathetic to teenaged wine bibbers. Anyone sophisticated or conservative looking was immediately ruled out, as were any old guys with gray hair or shiny heads, slacks or blazers, too.

This job required someone young and hip. Long hair, facial whiskers and worn out bell bottoms would identify the ideal candidate. After a few minutes, a shaggy hippy drifted out from the icehouse, his hippy-chick girlfriend clutched close to his side.

"Can you get some wine for us?" Jimmy begged, eyes drooping like a love-starved basset hound. The groovy couple was more than eager to oblige, but they thought it might look conspicuous if they went back in for a second purchase. Our new partner in crime came up with a plan and Jimmy and I climbed into the backseat of his rusty heap.

We rolled in front of another store and our bushy pal stuck his hand, open-palmed, over the tattered car bench. I thought he was giving me five—the ol' hippy handshake—so I slapped his palm with mine. "No, the money!" He quickly corrected me. Feeling like a complete idiot, I handed him the cash.

Once our flower children chauffeurs disappeared into the market, Jimmy let loose. He laughed and repeated, "No, the money!" over and over again. After about ten minutes of Jimmy busting his gut, the couple finally returned. They climbed in the beat up rattrap and presented us with a green bottle. It looked like an overgrown gourd with a large round base and a long narrow neck. The label said Spanada in big happy letters, and I knew this was quality stuff when I did not get change back for my $2 dollars.

After doing our evil bidding, our benefactors drove us to Sherman Oaks Park so Jimmy and I could offer toasts to peace, love and all that was groovy. We sat on a patch of grass, unscrewed the cap and shared the Hawaiian Punch of fine cabernets. The only things missing were candles and Englebert Humperdink crooning on a transistor radio.

We sipped into the evening's twilight, until only a lukewarm blend of sangria and backwash swirled in the bottom of our pretty glass gourd. All night Jimmy kept repeating, "No, the money!" then breaking out into hysterics.

The hour got late and the sky grew dark and eerie. With a half bottle of Spanada sloshing around in each of our bellies, Jimmy and I decided to roam the dim lit park. That's when we ran into two girls from school.

Neither Jimmy nor I had met them before, but we were very aware of their reputations. These were the girls moms warned their sons about. For one, their dress was extremely daring. Though ultra-revealing, their outfits did not appear to be a show of sensuality. There was a darker side to it, an act of defiance or a statement against social norms.

If their fashion statements were not shocking enough, they were also reputed to be witches. Just the kind of gals you want to run into late at night in the dark. These juvenile broom jockeys, Lisa and Diane, soon introduced us to an even drearier kind of darkness, one we really had no interest in.

They explained how their mothers taught them at young ages the art of witchcraft, including how to cast spells, and they gave us the names of people at school they pronounced curses upon. They told us how they plucked hair out of their unsuspecting victims' heads and used them in their efforts to inflict harm.

If that was not creepy enough, Jimmy and I totally freaked out when they presented their "Statement of Faith"—anti-faith and anti-Christ in the most literal sense. I did not know it at the time, but Satan worshippers have a gospel message of their own. It is one they even consider good news, but to the discerning, it is as damning as it is blasphemous.

Lisa told us Jesus was actually a son of Satan and that God was so jealous of the devil He went on a mad campaign to convince the world Christ was really His Son. She advocated the idea that God used the false promise of eternal life to lure people into following Him. I do not know if all Satanists believe this garbage, or if it is just some twisted lie propagated by some, but it was quite frightening and extremely disturbing to two sangria-intoxicated junior highers.

Admittedly, I was fully backslidden at this time, but God clearly had His hand upon me. As I listened to Lisa and Diane carry on with their satanic mumbo-jumbo, I sensed the presence of something, no, Someone more powerful than darkness. Though not at a place in my life where I pursued righteousness, I knew I did not want any of the sewage these girls spewed. I did not buy it. It stunk to high heaven, and the good Lord kept me from having anything to do with it.

God allowed me to toast the moonlight with a jug of sangria. He permitted me to pass out in my own puke, but no way was He handing off the pink slip to my soul.

Sometimes I think the greatest evidence for the existence of God is seeing what men reduce to when God is subtracted from their lives. I look back on what my life became when I walked away from the Lord, and I never want to go back to that place. I think instead on the forces of good and evil at work in our world, and choose to serve the One True and Living God. By His grace, I hope to extend a hand of Christian love to the lost, those people stumbling in the darkness, even if they happen to be little witches.

According to the "Quilt Code," the Drunkard's Path design instructs escapees to travel in a staggering fashion. Instead of moving in straight lines, it was recommended they meander and circle back over their tracks to confuse slave catchers who might be following them. This circuitous travel was also a hopeful attempt to throw dogs off their scents.

Also known as Wanderer in the Wilderness, some have linked this quilt pattern to a superstition. They believed a person sleeping under it might develop a thirst for drink and wonder away, and many refused to make the pattern for this reason.

Traditionally quilted in two fabrics, the Drunkard's Path has a symmetric, Celtic look. Swapping dark and light colors in rotation, the arrangement is sewn in a diagonal construction of a quarter-circle-in-a-square pattern—its undulating-all-over curved seams intimidating to beginning quilters.

Terry's tale of youthful inebriation easily lent itself to the title Drunkard's Path. In Terry's own words, he called himself backslidden, revealing a previous relationship with the Lord before his sangria-sodden adventure with Jimmy. So many of us, like Terry, travel twisted paths before coming, or returning to the Lord. Through every curve, every turn, and every steep place, God watches over us, allowing us to make our own decisions, yet ever ready to make Himself known. And God does send "red flags" into our lives—caution signs, yield signs, danger signs to protect us along the way. May we have the ears to listen and hearts to obey.

I once wrote a very amateurish little song based on Proverbs 4:18-19, a great Bible verse. "But the path of the just is as the shining light, that shineth more and more unto the perfect day. The way of the wicked is as darkness: they know not at what they stumble." It is a good thing to walk in the light, to be able to see the pitfalls ahead and avoid them. So let's walk in the light, and reach out a hand to those we meet along the way. And just in case you like to indulge in a corny song from time to time, I'll share mine here.

Walk On

I'm gonna walk on, walk on, walk on
I'm gonna walk on, walk, on, walk on
I'm walking on the path to victory
The road of sin is the road of death
So I'll walk with Jesus 'til I draw my last breath
I'm walking on the path to victory

The road the righteous travel is like the sunrise
Getting' brighter, brighter brighter 'til the daylight comes
But the road of the wicked is as a dark night
They can't see so they stumble and fall

I'm gonna walk on, walk on, walk on
I'm gonna walk on, walk, on, walk on
I'm walking on the path to victory
The road of sin is the road of death
So I'll walk with Jesus 'til I draw my last breath
I'm walking on the path to victory

Flee from sin and fear the Lord
Walk humbly before Him and obey His commands
Dwell together in unity
Worship in one accord
And walk in victory

I'm gonna walk on, walk on, walk on
I'm gonna walk on, walk, on, walk on
I'm walking on the path to victory

The road of sin is the road of death,
So I'll walk with Jesus 'til I draw my last breath
I'm walking on the path to victory

CHAPTER 11
STARS

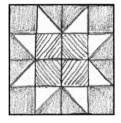

Claudia Gajewski – Beverly Hills, Michigan

My emotions are tangoing in a lively variance of steps and poses. One takes the lead, then a quick spin, and then another sends me off in a completely different direction. I am nervous, but more than anything, excited and hopeful. The last time—my third time facing this procedure—I passed the waiting period binding my Rivers of Life quilt. I made the quilt in just three weeks and used a quick basting stitch to finish it off a mere 24 hours before my surgery.

Tomorrow, I undergo the same procedure, and as I think about the event and all the possible outcomes, my quilt comes to mind. Quilts are special. More than blankets, quilts are warmth, protection, beautiful works of art, works of heart, and for some, records of events.

I share a love for quilting with my mother-in-law, Alice. She retired from a demanding career as the head of hospital infection control to quilt. Before she retired, when stress became heavy at work, she visited the fabric store for therapy. Just running her hands over different fabrics—the tactile sense alone—was enough to calm her and release the tension of her days. Perhaps I followed her example when I dove into the quilting project prior to my last procedure.

The primary colors I chose: oranges and reds with yellow and pink highlights, related in my mind to the beginning of life. In addition to the vibrant colors, I also chose some dark ones—reds and purples—reminders that sometimes life starts, but then stops. I knew well the possibilities. Not every life begun makes its way into our world.

Our first attempt at introcytoplasmic sperm injection (ISP), an in vitro fertilization procedure, failed. The second time a tiny, fighter, four-celled embryo grew into a beautiful baby girl. We were thrilled. Two years later, in hopes of giving Emily a sibling, we faced in vitro again. That time our whole family walked with us on our medical journey, including the making of the quilt.

The pattern was simple: eight-inch by eight-inch flannel squares, nine across and seven down, but the quilt was vibrant. Without the use of sashing, colorful block butted up against colorful block, each pigment representing one of the many details I was coping with at that time in my life—my husband, our 20-month-old daughter, family expectations, household obligations, daily injections, office visits, co-pays, blood draws, counseling, and the list went on.

To offset the riot of color, I made a one-inch stop border of black with double-paired cherries. Following the black band, I added two more bands of the lead colors: a half-inch of orange star fabric and a half-inch of red, a dramatic outer frame. The final band, black with a subtle raspberry pattern, I nicknamed "midnight raspberries," and for the backing, I chose a black fabric with a celestial pattern with gold and silver accents. The fruit patterns represented the fruit of my womb and the fruit of my labors.

Married at the age of 22 to a healthy man of 23, I never imagined my husband and I would have problems conceiving. To our surprise, we fought infertility for twelve years before Emily's birth. Over the years, as we worked so hard at "creating," I included my own crafty creativity in the process. I made a pin-back button that I wore to the first in vitro fertilization procedure. The second time, I got more creative—a lab coat and scrubs for my favorite Beanie Baby, Velvet, who went with me to the clinic. Third time, quilt time, we were so pumped up we included the family.

With the positive results of the last procedure, all had been hopeful it would work again. As I prepared, I looked at photos taken of me making the quilt with everyone helping and watching. Alice and my sister-in-law Kim had helped me prepare the fabric, cutting material with a rotary cutter and giving me advice. Even the men pitched in. My husband and father-in-law helped me pin the quilt, chatting while we worked together.

All went well the day of the procedure. I received two excellent embryos and froze the third. My family was ecstatic when I became pregnant, but from the beginning, I had a niggling feeling things would not end as we all hoped. When our beloved reproductive endocrinologist (who had been with us since the beginning) told us we were pregnant, it was on the tip of my tongue to say, "This is a mistake."

In spite of morning sickness and fatigue, I carried a feeling the pregnancy was not viable. At three weeks, we saw the baby's heart beat, then slowly all symptoms disappeared. I miscarried on Father's Day, two months later.

My mother-in-law once showed me a quilt made in the 1800s by a woman grieving the loss of her daughter. With clarity, I recognized the grief poured out in every stitch. In designing my quilt, I had been realistic about what could happen. I included dark squares of purple and blackish maroon—blood, bleeding, the end of a life beginning. I stared at the dark squares. I flipped the quilt over and the back seemed a black celestial space on the bed. I thought about my baby, somewhere in space, comforted by thoughts that he was in heaven. Funny, but I felt certain I had a boy and later medical testing confirmed it.

When I prepared to back my Rivers of Life quilt, I learned a lesson about complete faith. I had searched for the right place to cut the material, hemming and hawing over where to put the straight seam, all under Alice's watchful gaze. "Just rip it," she said. I looked at her in horror, but she knew what she was saying. "If the fabric is good, the rip will divide cleanly," she assured, so I put my faith in the master quilter and handed her my scissors. After a small snip, she grabbed the fabric and rent it cleanly in two pieces.

Faith plays a big part in facing tomorrow. We only froze one embryo. There was only one to freeze, the smallest one. I put all my faith in this one chance—my one snip and let it rip. I have prepared myself for disappointment and realize my chances are slim.

My husband and I have kept tomorrow's procedure our secret. Family expectations can be very weighty and looking back on the last incident I realized I spent myself managing the needs of others instead of doing what I needed for myself.

Calm. That's what I need to cope. This is our fourth attempt. I have my Rivers of Life quilt out and ready to go, and I hope for a child from the Lord, but all I have ever prayed for is grace for whatever comes.

⚜

Ozella's "Quilt Code" concluded with a Stars pattern. The *Encyclopedia of Pieced Quilt Patterns* by Barbara Brackman lists the word "star" 269 times, indicating the popularity of stars in hearts and handiwork. Although the star pattern referenced by Ozella does not necessarily indicate the North Star, it is said to instruct fleeing slaves to look toward the heavens for direction. The North Star, one of the most easily identifiable stars in our hemisphere, has guided travelers for millennia.

In the North Star quilt pattern, eight triangles surround a center square to form a star shape. Numerous variations of the pattern exist, including a beautiful North Star Compass whose name bears a compound message of guidance from the heavens.

Runaway slaves fled their masters' homes, taking risks with faith and fear and no certainty of achieving their goals of freedom. This reminded me of Claudia's brave journey. An entry in my prayer journal says, "Calm is trust in action," and when I look at the elements of Claudia's story, her faith, her resolve and the peace in which she faces an uncertain future, I am encouraged to face my own unknowns in the same noble manner.

The dark backing of her quilt dotted with gold and silver orbs and stars, connects Claudia's story to the Stars quilt design. The dark celestial pattern comforted Claudia with a reminder that her beloved child lived on in heaven. Claudia's story, one that keeps us hanging and hoping with her, seems to conclude without a resolution, but she leaves us with a powerful message—"pray for grace for whatever comes."

CHAPTER 12
THE BIG DIPPER

Troy Butler – Troy, Michigan

"I'm sorry, Mrs. Butler, but your child will most likely be stillborn. If not, I don't expect him to live more than an hour." Those are not the words a laboring mother wants to hear, but they are what my mother heard 41 years ago. I thank God for my life, although it has come with the challenges of living with cerebral palsy—the day-to-day physical difficulties, compounded by the emotional aspects of disability,

As a child, I struggled with people and friends accepting me. Three days a week I attended a preschool program at the Easter Seals center where I had speech and language therapy, occupational therapy and physical therapy. When I was four, two of my classmates died of cancer. I remember distinctly the anxiety and fear that became a part of my life after they passed.

With my type of cerebral palsy, I have no sense of balance or control. When I was five, I sneezed and fell out of my wheelchair, breaking the wrist caught under my mom's bed. I think that experience contributed to the intense fear of falling I carried for so many years.

Life went on, with its fears and challenges. I graduated from college and began a desperate search to find myself. My dad had been sick for 11 years. His kidneys were failing, a complication of diabetes. As his condition worsened, I found myself growing angry with God.

The Lord used a young man, Brandon McKenzie, to reach to me with a life-changing message. Brandon came to me through Home Health Outreach as a hired attendant. My parents were not very happy with Brandon. Their personalities clashed. I thought he was a little strange—actually, a lot strange. But there was something enticing about the way he did things. He had a confidence I had never experienced before. My family and I did not really know what to think of Brandon, but after a month or two, I knew I wanted more of what he had, God living inside him.

My first introduction to his church was on October 2, 1998. I visited with the expectations of demonstrating my service dog, Tug, but, oh boy, the Lord had other plans unbeknownst to me. The pastor, the late Rev. Mark Reed, was teaching about the Holy Ghost. I know the Bible study was for the whole church, but it was as if he was talking right to me. In the middle of my pain and searching, the Lord used his message to open a new door for me and my life has never been the same.

It was that night and the nights that followed I began to experience freedom in Jesus I had never known before. I was raised in a traditional Protestant faith that did not teach the infilling of the Holy Ghost. I had been baptized previously, but I knew I wanted to be baptized again, this time in Jesus' name. It took several men from the church to carry me and lower me into the baptismal tank. Two of them assisted me in the tank, and when I was lifted out of the water, I came out speaking in a language I had never known. I felt a peace come over my life and found what I was looking for in God.

In my relationship with Brandon, I have learned many things, not all of them spiritual. Once I was due to give a report for a class. Brandon dared me to give my report and skip the rest of the class, so after I gave the report I told the instructor I had to leave. Brandon took me to the mall. I was new in the church and excited about leaving cards everywhere to witness to people. Brandon and his brother wheeled me into Victoria's Secret and put a church card on a lingerie-clad mannequin. He turned me around to face the mannequin and said, "Pastor and Sister Reed are right there, and they're going to get you…ha, ha, ha." I was mortified until I realized he was kidding. Brandon was always up to mischief and enticing me to push the envelope, but it has been worth the ride.

Since my baptism and infilling of the Spirit of God, my life has a whole new meaning. I am free to worship and share God with others.

It is exciting to live for God, even in a wheelchair. I have often heard people, with and without disabilities, say, "Why me, Lord?" When I look up to heaven, I have to say, "Why not me?" Jesus died for me, and that is more than enough. Living with the joy and beauty of salvation and His love fills my heart with thanksgiving, and it is all because of Him.

"Why did this happen to you? To your family?" people have asked. I understand the questions, but I have to say I would rather be in this chair with the Lord than out of it without Him. 1 Peter 5:7 talks about casting all our cares upon the Lord because He cares for us. I rest on that verse often and pray, "Lord, I am giving my cares up to You." If I held on to them, life would be so much harder and I would be in so much more pain than I have now.

The world is full of pain, but I refuse to let my body be a detriment to my service to God. I take every day as it comes and have learned to roll with the circumstances I face. I give my struggles to God the minute they happen, knowing I can't do it, but He can. He helps me face my mountains and think of them as mole hills. He turns my adversities into joy.

The Lord has opened many doors for me to minister within the church teaching Sunday School and greeting, serving on boards as an advocate for the disability community and at disability camps I attend. Over 41 years have passed since the gloomy report from my mother's doctor, and here I am, alive and serving the Lord. The fears that once plagued my life no longer control me, because I know that God is in control and I have freedom in my life with Him.

The Big Dipper quilt block, a four-patch design that uses two colors of half-square triangles and triangles, is an old favorite. The motif sets a pinwheel on a corner and surrounds the diamond shape with a bi-colored set of triangles in each corner. Not directly attributed as one used in the "Underground Railroad Quilt Code," the Big Dipper relates to the Star pattern discussed in the previous chapter.

Runaway slaves often traveled by night. The easily recognizable form of the Big Dipper pointed them to the North Star, a celestial navigational tool and guiding light that directed them to freedom in Canada.

Further connecting the Big Dipper, also known as the Drinking Gourd, to the efforts of freedom, many historians believe the song Follow the Drinking Gourd outlined directions to the Underground Railroad. H.B. Parks, a Texas entomologist and amateur folklorist, claimed the song encoded traveling instructions that mapped a route from Mobile, Alabama, to where the Tennessee and Ohio rivers meet in my home town, Paducah, Kentucky—a place most quilters know as the quilt capital of the world.

My husband was privileged to be one of the men in the water the night Troy was baptized. He helped carry him in and held him throughout the process, an experience none of us will ever forget.

Although I grew up attending church on a regular basis, it was not until I was an adult I learned what the Bible teaches about baptism. In 1561, due to pressure from those favoring sprinkling over immersion, Bible translators refrained from translating the Greek word baptizo into English. Instead, they created a new word: baptize. Adopting this new word had no effect on its meaning, which is and ever will be to dip. And that's what Troy did. He made a big dip that made a big difference in his life, and his testimony and cheerful spirit continue to make a difference in the lives of all those he meets.

CHAPTER 13
SAILBOAT

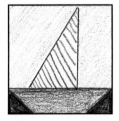

Anne McManus – Rochester Hills, Michigan

My grandmother had 12 grandchildren—a piece of information she liked to include with every introduction. Usually at lunch, to our waiter or waitress, she would say, "These are 3 of my 12 grandchildren," or whatever number was the appropriate one at the time. Every one of us knew, without a doubt, that Granny loved us and she was pleased to have us with her that day. She nurtured in me a feeling of family and acceptance I have always cherished.

Granny spent time with her grandchildren during the years when we were young. Every December she drove us to see the shopping mall decked out in Christmas lights and finery. During summer holidays, we went on excursions to count the cars at the Forest Preserve parks. It was a simple outing, but just being with Granny made it special.

Some Saturdays Granny took us out to lunch at a restaurant near her apartment. I will never forget those times. I almost always ordered a hot dog, French fries, coleslaw and a chocolate malt. Granny never ordered French fries or malts for herself, she was always on a diet, but she usually helped us finish ours.

Apart from other family get-togethers, these outings with Granny had a sameness to them that was reassuring to me. I enjoyed each one, but of all the places we traveled, my favorite outing was to the cemetery to "feed the swans."

Granny saved leftover bread in a plastic bag just for this purpose. I looked forward to the days she took me on this special trip. Granny would grab her bag of bread, collect a few of her grandchildren, and then drive us to the cemetery.

The cemetery was a beautiful place. A large pond lay in the center surrounded by a variety of trees. Our family burial plot, next to the pond, was my grandfather's resting place, as well as that of an infant born to my grandmother's niece, and one belonging to her brother.

Year after year, we returned and fed the wild swans that lived around the pond. Granny ended each visit standing near the gravestone of her husband. Many years had passed since his death in 1937 at the age of 46. Still, Granny loved standing there. She would look fondly at the stone, and I can still hear her in my mind saying, "Oh, I miss him terribly and I can't wait to see him again!"

Now, many years later, both my parents are buried in the cemetery along with my grandmother and grandfather. During a recent visit with my son, the idea came to me to make crayon and paper rubbings of the grave markers to take to our home out-of-state. We grabbed paper and crayons, whatever we had, and hurriedly made six rubbings of the stones, not thinking about the color choices or any particular technique.

When we returned from our trip, I had the rubbings framed, and the colorful images of my relatives' stones now hang in a corner upstairs in my home. I like looking at them—the identical sizes, the typefaces and of course the names of the people I love in vibrant shades of magenta, lime, orange, turquoise and purple. I like remembering the day I spent making them with my son, not knowing their importance at the time.

Now I know how Granny felt. I, too, miss my family terribly and can't wait to see them again. When I look at the rubbings, I think about Granny and the seed of faith she planted in my heart as a little girl. Faith took root and grew—a faith that now reassures me I will meet my loved ones again, not by a swan-filled pond surrounded by trees, but by the crystal pure waters of the river of life that flow to the tree of eternal life and the throne of God.

Sailboat quilt blocks look like juvenile drawings of their namesakes with simple triangular sails attached to trapezoid boats. The pattern was said to be a symbol of safe water passage for escaping slaves on canoes, barges, steamships or rafts. Free black sailors and ship owners hid refugees on board their vessels and then transported them to freedom in Canada. After the Fugitive Slave Act passed in 1850, escaped slaves found in free states were in jeopardy of being returned to their owners, often at the hands of ruthless bounty hunters. The passing of this act made it necessary for runaways to continue their journeys beyond the free northern states and into Canada. This was often accomplished by means of water travel.

The Sailboat pattern relates well to Anne's story. First, the simplicity of the design, often made in bright colors for children's blankets, seemed a good fit with the colorful crayon rubbings Anne made with her son. Secondly, at the cemetery, the place Anne remembered her loved ones and their passages to their new heavenly home, the swans gliding across the pond brought to mind visions of sailboats skimming across the sea, transporting their passengers to destinations unknown.

I thought the crayon rubbings were a great idea, and when I saw them in Anne's home, I asked her to share their story. The vibrant framed images, tangible connections to those who have already passed from our natural world into the supernatural, are soul warming delights. Remembrances of life—remembrances of loss—papers bearing colorful images of granite stones keep memories near and remind Anne, as well as those of us reading here, of our hope to meet our loved ones again—free from pain, free from loss—in our eternal home with Jesus.

"No man can put a chain about the ankle of his fellow man without at last finding the other end fastened about his own neck."
— Frederick Douglass, speech, Civil Rights Mass Meeting, Washington, D.C., 1883

CHAPTER 14
CATCH ME IF YOU CAN

Jacquelin Harris – Englewood, Ohio

We lived in Knob Noster, Missouri, near Whiteman Air Force Base where my husband was stationed in the United States Air Force. One summer I discovered an orange tabby cat living in the wooded area behind our house. It was obvious from his appearance he was not well. He was so thin – his emaciated body, topped with a head that seemed made for a much larger cat, gave him a bobble-head look. One of his eyes was damaged and I wondered if he might be blind in one eye.

I love cats and just could not bear the thought of the poor animal suffering, so I bought some cat food and began my mission to reach out to the downtrodden feline. Daily I walked out on the concrete slab in our back yard with a dish of food. He ran off every time he saw me. Disappointed, I would put the food down and go back in house where I watched him eat from the window.

This went on for a few weeks. Little by little, he stayed nearer to the house. I kept my distance, but spoke to him gently. Over time, he came to trust me.

One day after he finished eating, he stretched out at the end of the concrete slab and fell asleep. Quiet as a mouse, I sat on the concrete beside him, reached over, and ever so gently stroked his back. He opened his eyes and I sat up quickly, pulling away, not knowing if I might be bitten or scratched. Instead of running away, the cat stood and climbed in my lap. He pressed his head against my chin and gave me a kitty hug with a loud purr.

After he put some weight on, he became quite a handsome fellow. We named him Morris. Over time, he grew so big we affectionately called him Morrisaurus.

Once we earned the cat's trust and he gained ours, my husband and I took him to the veterinarian. With his new steady diet of good food, his health was much improved from when we had first seen the poor malnourished creature. The vet treated him for a severe case of ear mites and we learned his second eyelid was damaged, but he was not blind, and we were thankful for that. Happily, we took Morris home and then he really became an official part of our family.

We settled in, glad to have our new pet with us. As we returned home, I felt the Lord prompt me to reflect on the way we had gained Morris' affection and trust—how the experience of winning a cat might relate to the way Christians interact with the lost and each other.

Many Christians are reluctant to reach out to the hurting people around them. We excuse our lack of interaction with an excuse—considering the "disease of sin" has damaged the sense of reasoning in the heart of those who do not know God. Although unbelievers may not understand the Scriptures we quote, and they may have trouble seeing the answer for their aching souls, they are not blind to genuine godly compassion.

Initially, no matter how we may try to help or reach out, the hurting may reject us or even run away. Many simply do not know how to respond to sincere love or kindness. With Morris, it took time, effort, the cost of cat food and many acts of consistent kindness to make him believe I cared and would not hurt him. Those who seem to push us away may need that same kind of investment—consistent kindness in their lives. It is not easy. We have to take the risk that we might get bit or scratched by cruel words or unkind attitudes, but it is worth the effort to bring a new life into the family of God. Are we willing to look beyond the dangers and reach for the soul?

I love cats, they fascinate me, and I think they are some of God's most beautiful creations. Personally, I have had to pray for that kind of love for people. Through prayer, God has changed me and helped me grow in this area. I now look forward to visiting the nursing home or the children's hospital. I especially love teaching Sunday School and helping with our Ladies Auxiliary.

Jesus reached out to those in need. In Matthew 8:2-3, the Word says , "And, behold, there came a leper and worshipped him, saying Lord if thou wilt, thou canst make me clean. And Jesus put forth his hand, and touched him saying, I will, be thou clean. And immediately his leprosy was cleansed."

I have often wondered how long it might have been since the leper had felt the caring touch of another human being. Before Jesus healed the man of his contagious deadly disease, He touched him. Under the Jewish law, this simple touch would have made Jesus "unclean," but Jesus came proclaiming a better law—the law of kindness. The leper was touched by perfect love, perfect peace and perfect power, and then Jesus healed him.

It is not only sinners who need the love of God extended to them. Our brothers and sisters in the Lord often come into church carrying horrific pains from their pasts, struggles in the present and worries for the future. The baggage people bring with them can make it difficult for fellow Christians to take others at face value, but we can all show brotherly affection and do our parts to build up the Body of Christ.

If I had fed Morris only a couple of times, or if he never responded to my touch, he might still be starving or even dead. The Word of God says, "And (add) to godliness brotherly kindness; and to brotherly kindness charity" (2 Peter 1:7). Consistent kindness may cost us something, but it could liberate a soul from death to life. Led by the Holy Ghost and touched by the healing balm of His love, God's children overcome and can help others do the same. When we offer God's love to others, He will draw them to Himself and extend to them the opportunity to walk in newness of life in Christ.

❧ ❧

The Catch Me If You Can quilt block, also known as Flyfoot, is an old design dated back to 1935. Quilt historian Barbara Brackman made the following comment about the design: "This pattern can remind us of the Underground Railroad when escaping slaves ran to freedom. Although the block's name is a twentieth century invention, the lively image seems to capture the cleverness such a journey required." The pattern name, Catch Me If You Can, certainly gives a glimpse into the determination required by those who risked their all to run for freedom.

Two colors of simple triangles form what looks to be a complex pattern, a swastika shape of spinning blades or pinwheels. The same motif has also been made with rectangles. I found it interesting the triangle version of the Catch Me If You Can quilt is made of eight Flying Geese, a pattern we already discussed in Chapter 9. That is the way God works, isn't it? He takes the lessons learned through one experience and uses them to show us something new in another. Serving God is never boring.

Jacquelin faced a bit of danger when she reached out to Morris. She took a risk the cat might injure her. Morris was caught, however, eventually snagged with a hook of kindness on a line of love that reeled the sick, lonely feline into a relationship that provided healing, shelter and companionship. Jacquelin and Morris were both rewarded by Jacquelin's efforts—her fruit of the Spirit on display. Including peace, joy, goodness, patience, kindness, and mercy, the fruit of the Spirit in Jacquelin's life were not hanging on a tree for her pleasure, but to nourish the lives of those around her—even the life of a cat.

OK. Now for the truth. I admit it. I am not a cat person. I am not a dog person. I am not a hamster or fish person. I am not a pet person at all, but I learned a lot from Jacquelin's experience and her insightful reflection and application. Thanks, Jacquelin.

CHAPTER 15
BRIGHT HOPES

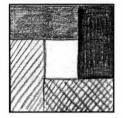

Dr. Helen Roseveare – Holywood, North Ireland

O ne night in Central Africa, I worked for hours in the labor ward helping a mother as she delivered her child. In spite of all our efforts, the poor woman died leaving behind a tiny, premature baby and a crying, two-year-old daughter.

We knew we faced difficulty keeping the baby alive. We had no incubator. We had no electricity to run an incubator or any special feeding facilities, and although we lived on the equator, nights were often chilly and drafts treacherous.

A student-midwife went for the box of supplies we kept for premature babies and for the cotton wool we would wrap the infant in. Another left to stoke up the fire and fill the hot water bottle we used to keep babies warm. She came back shortly, distressed, and told me that while she was filling the bottle, it had burst. "...and it is our last hot water bottle!" she exclaimed.

Rubber perishes easily in tropical climates. In the West, the saying goes it is no good crying over spilled milk; in Central Africa it might be considered no good crying over burst water bottles. They do not grow on trees, and there are no drugstores down forest pathways. "All right," I said. "Put the baby as near the fire as you safely can and sleep between the baby and the door to keep it from the drafts. Your job is to keep the baby warm."

The following noon, as I did most days, I went to have prayers with many of the orphanage children. Many often chose to gather with me and I gave the youngsters various suggestions of things to pray about and told them about the tiny baby. I explained our problem about keeping the baby warm enough, mentioning the hot water bottle and how the baby could so easily die if it got chilled. I also told them about the two-year-old sister crying because her mother had died.

During the prayer time, Ruth, a ten-year-old girl, prayed with the usual blunt consciousness of our African children. "Please, God," she said, "send us a water bottle. It'll be no good tomorrow, God, the baby'll be dead; so, please send it this afternoon."

While I gasped inwardly at the audacity of the prayer, she added by way of corollary, "...And while You are about it, would You please send a dolly for the little girl so she'll know You really love her?"

As often with children's prayers, I was put on the spot. Could I honestly say, "Amen?" I just did not believe that God could do this. Oh, yes, I knew that He could do anything: the Bible says so, but there are limits, aren't there?

The only way I imagined God might answer this particular prayer would be through a parcel from the homeland. I had been in Africa for almost four years and I had never, ever received a parcel from home. And, I imagined, if anyone did send a parcel, who would think of including a hot water bottle? We lived on the equator!

Halfway through the afternoon, while I taught in the nurses' training school, a message arrived. A car was at my front door. By the time I reached home, the car had gone, but there on the veranda, was a large 22 pound parcel! Tears pricked my eyes. I could not open the parcel alone, so I sent for the orphanage children. Together we pulled off the string, carefully undoing each knot. We folded the paper, taking care not to tear it unduly.

Excitement was mounting. Some thirty or forty pairs of eyes were focused on the large cardboard box. From the top, I lifted out brightly colored knit jerseys. Eyes sparkled as I gave them out to the children around me. After the tops, I pulled out knit bandages for the leprosy patients. The children were a little bored with this, but next came a box of mixed raisins and sultanas—these would make a nice batch of buns for the weekend.

As I put my hand in again, I felt the...could it really be? I grasped it, and pulled it out.

"A brand-new rubber hot water bottle!" I cried.

I had not asked God to send it; I had not truly believed that He could. Ruth was in the front row of the children. She rushed forward, crying out, "If God has sent the bottle, He must have sent the dolly, too!"

Rummaging down to the bottom of the box, she pulled out a small, beautifully dressed dolly. Her eyes shone: She had never doubted! Looking up at me, she asked, "Can I go over with you, Mummy, and give this dolly to that little girl, so she'll know that Jesus really loves her?"

That parcel had been on its way for five months. Packed and sent by my former Sunday School class, the leader had heard and obeyed God's prompting to send a hot water bottle. One of the girls included the dolly for an African child—five months earlier to answer to the believing prayer of a ten-year-old to bring it "that afternoon!"

"And it shall come to pass, that before they call, I will answer; and while they are yet speaking, I will hear" (Isaiah 65:24).

⟅⟆

The Bright Hopes quilt pattern, a variation of a traditional nine-patch block, features a light patch in the middle of darkness. Surrounding a center square, four rectangles march in progression from medium-light to dark. Sewn together, the design looks somewhat like boxes stacked in neat rows, bringing to mind the parcel in Helen's story.

When researching Bright Hopes' connection with slavery and possibly the Underground Railroad, I found the following account written in the *New York Herald*, The Underground Railroad, August 14, 1859 (typographical errors preserved):

> ...Mr. Still, of Philadelphia, addressed an audience on the present condition and prospects of the underground railroad...On the 4th of July last...fugitives from the southern shore of Maryland, with bitter haired for slavery and bright hopes for Canada, passed along the road...One had recently arrived at Philadelphia in a box so short that he could not lie his length...

Now that's a package almost as surprising as the one Helen received in Africa. The passion and hope that inspired a man to ship himself in a box from a slave state to free state must have been some kind of special hope indeed. Surely he stepped in the container with prayer and continued to pray with each strike of the hammer that secured the lid for shipment.

Just as surely, little Ruth's prayers for the new orphans touched the heart of God. He reached outside of time, and in His wonderful way set the wheels in motion to meet the needs to come in another country five months in advance.

When we understand and embrace our omnipresent, omnipotent God's ability and power to miraculously provide in seemingly impossible situations, we receive a truly liberating gift. Free from dependency upon our own power and resources, we have access to so much more than our limited means and abilities.

Looking beyond time is nothing new to God. From the foundation of the world, before time began, Jesus is...and Jesus is our hope (1 Timothy 1:1). God wrapped Himself in the package of a mortal man, walked the earth among His creation, and offered His life that others might live. From the cross, Jesus saw us—you and me, beyond time, beyond the physical realm. That's our God...sending a package of bright hope to mankind in Jesus (Isaiah 9:6).

CHAPTER 16
BEACON LIGHT

Kim Zaksek – Poland, Ohio

One evening in 1990, in the days before remote controls, I turned the dial on my television set looking for a program that caught my attention. I settled on *20/20* and then snuggled in to my couch to watch a documentary, Shame of a Nation. I loved learning about new places, and watched with interest the images that crossed the screen, pictures that etched deeply in my heart and mind and ultimately changed my life.

The people of Romania had recently won their freedom from communist rule. Stripped of their liberty and culture under Nicolae Ceausescu's leadership, many had suffered under the greed and evil of his regime—children most of all. When Romania finally opened its doors for the world to see, over one hundred thousand children were found abandoned in deplorable conditions in state-run institutions. The footage was heartbreaking: naked children housed in large groups, babies lined on tiered carts like loaves of bread. Their eyes were hollow, their stares blank. In that moment I knew I was being called to save a child.

Several years later my husband and I traveled to Romania to bring our first child home—a beautiful boy with big brown eyes and wavy brown hair. After spending his first 6 weeks in a maternity hospital, he had been transported to an orphanage where he lived for 19 months. One look at this child, and we immediately fell in love. It must have shown on my face. My husband says to this day, "You were glowing." After an appointment at a local clinic, a trip to the embassy, and a bit of sightseeing, we began our journey home—a family. It was a journey filled with emotional twists and turns, but one I would not change for anything.

Our son, quiet and timid, welcomed our love and comfort. He enjoyed being held and rocked as he played with blocks and looked at books. Our life seemed typical. I thought we were all happy, but after a six-month honeymoon, things began to change. My son's emotions and reactions to everyday situations became more and more difficult—over the top, I thought. Conventional parenting did not work. As a mother and former educator, I knew something was wrong and sought outside help, scared and unsure what the future held.

Therapy appointments and at-home exercises filled our days. Every day I struggled to do my best for my son and maintain a peaceful home for my husband and new daughter. Anxiety became part of my makeup and sent me on a downward spiral.

I suffered physically from the stress. After months of losing weight, panic attacks, and compulsive symptoms, my husband and I met with our family doctor. He told us the special needs of a child are often trying for a family, especially the primary caregiver, and he recommended counseling. We followed his advice, and one week later I began seeing a therapist. Faithfully I went for one year, then another. I was taken on an unforgettable journey into my past where I faced my own feelings of abandonment, isolation, fear, and shame. Abandonment, isolation, and fear—the same wounds I had been trying to heal in my son.

Twice each week I attended sessions. I kept a journal, and worked as hard as I could to heal. The revelation I gained through these sessions and exercises brought some healing, yet a part of me still struggled, until one day…

It was a cold January morning. My husband stayed home with the children who were sick. Alone, I walked into church, a new one that was very different from the church I attended as a child. The sermon spoke to me personally, and the pastor concluded with an invitation to pray at the altar. Tears streamed down my face. I knew God was reaching to me. When I arrived at the altar a lovely woman approached me, but shame overtook my mind and I was unable to speak. She began praying and her words seemed as though she had walked alongside me on my journey. She prayed for peace in my mind. She spoke of faith and the power of Jesus Christ. My head spun, but within moments I felt an incredible sense of peace. It was as though the burden I carried for so long finally lifted and Jesus, the Lord and Savior, lived inside of me.

A few weeks later my husband also came to know the Lord and we began praying for our son. As a mother, I wanted to ask Jesus to be my son's Savior, to actually do it for him, but I could not and so my husband and I prayed. I often asked him, "Are you ready yet?" and received a "not yet" in response.

We had been in church for two years when we decided to attend a free creation seminar hosted at a local church. My son loves science and animals, and the first morning session, filled with facts and fun, kept him glued to the screen. At its conclusion, the man presenting invited those who did not know Jesus to ask Him into their hearts. Heads bowed and eyes closed, we listened as many children began to pray. Then I heard a small voice, the one I had been praying for, and tears filled my eyes. My son, who had suffered so much from the pain of abandonment and loss, asked Jesus to be his Savior! Layers of heartache peeled away. My son had Jesus and I knew he was going to be okay.

When we returned home, my son disappeared into his room to sort out his science and animal books, one pile for truth and the other for manmade truths. He donated the books to the creation speaker that evening to use as examples in his presentations and I watched in awe.

Today I am still in awe of the love of God and how He saves. John 3:16-17 (NIV) says, "For God so loved the world that he gave his one and only Son, that whoever believes in him shall not perish, but have eternal life. For God did not send his Son into the world to condemn the world, but to save the world through him." In my effort to save a child, first from a Romanian orphanage, then from emotional distress, I learned there is only One who can truly save. His name is Jesus, and I am so glad He still saves today.

Variations of the Beacon Light quilt pattern all begin with a center square that is surrounded by squares, rectangles, or a combination of both that form an outer square. Sitting on the point of a right angle, one bold variation adds three-piece units at the corners of the diamond creating a cross pattern out of colored triangles. Another sets the square in triangles making star blocks.

The Beacon Light pattern represents Ripley, Ohio, one of the major stops on the Underground Railroad. An abolitionist, Reverend John Rankin, upon his move to Ripley became one of the free state's first and most active conductors. His home, situated at the top of a 540-foot hill, provided a wide view of the village, the Ohio River and the Kentucky shoreline. A lantern raised on a flagpole indicated to fleeing slaves when passage across the river was safe. Rankin also built a staircase leading up the hill, a path two thousand refugees used to escape through his home.

In his "I Have A Dream" speech in 1963, Martin Luther King cited the Emancipation Proclamation as a "momentous decree...a great beacon light of hope to millions...a joyous daybreak to end the long night of captivity." As in the times of Reverend Rankin and Doctor King, the light of God's Word still provides a beacon to searching hearts.

Kim's journey, beginning with compassion kindled for lost children in need, took her on a journey across continents and into a new light in her relationship with God. I pray that our churches, and you and I (the Church), shine with the light of the Gospel of Truth pulsing through the darkness, guiding the hearts of weary travelers on their paths to freedom in Jesus.

CHAPTER 17
COURTHOUSE STEPS

Carol McCartney — Bloomfield Hills, Michigan

Not long ago our family experienced a real-life, modern-day David and Goliath battle. In my opinion, the final outcome was just as spectacular as the biblical version.

Twenty years ago, my husband and three business partners formed a company to sell and repair mechanical seals. They enjoyed a steady and consistent business, and the company provided a good home to the 15 employees who worked there. Over the years, the company took on the feel of a family business and my husband took his fatherly role very serious. His compassion and sense of fairness were well recognized throughout the shop.

In 2004, my husband and his partners found themselves in the middle of a lawsuit, totally unprepared for what lay ahead. The more entangled we became in the judicial system, the more it seemed like a sausage factory. And as they say about sausage, you just do not want to know what goes into it.

We were being sued by a Goliath—a $2 billion dollar company who alleged our business illegally represented ourselves as producers of their product.

The process for repairing mechanical seals is much the same across the country and around the world. A customer sends the repair shop a mechanical seal in a box (many times the manufacturer's box). Our company repairs the seals and ships them back to the customers in the same boxes we received them in. On the box we place a new label that reads, "Repaired by <u>Business Name</u>)."

So here we are, going about our simple, day-to-day business operations, and out of nowhere this lawsuit hits. At first, we did not take it as a serious threat. We could not fathom someone suing us for using the same return mail procedure used by most everyone in the repair business. Shops all over the world repair items manufactured by others and return them to their customers in bags or boxes marked with the name of the repairer.

Ignoring the problem, however, did nothing to remove it, and very quickly we found ourselves face-to-face with the stark and brutal reality that anyone, anywhere, can allege you have committed some wrong, some crime, some illegal act—and the burden is on you to prove that you did not. If you do not fight to prove your innocence, the results can be catastrophic.

The ensuing legal battle raged on, and our little company spent huge dollars for our attorney's expertise. Day after day, week after week, month after month, the battle continued, the weight growing heavier and heavier. My husband worked often throughout the day and then into the night trying to make sure all the 'truth' was communicated effectively through the legal process. At the same time, he worked feverishly to keep the company viable and maintain jobs for our employees.

We made it through the first two years, but late one night as I sat with my husband going over the details of the current state of the lawsuit, something broke, and I cried out with a broken heart, "It's just not fair! How can they do this to people who have not done anything wrong?" My sense of justice was wounded at its core.

The next morning I realized something I had never known before I became involved in this lawsuit. God truly listens to our cries, and He comes to our aid.

As was my custom, at 5:00 a.m., I settled myself into my morning devotion. I cherished the time with my Lord in prayer, Bible reading, contemplation and listening. This particular morning the Lord led me to Psalm 9. I was reading from "The Message," and when I read the words, there was no mistaking the message God spoke to me. The words leapt off the page.

This was the first time in my Christian journey I experienced such a drawing to one passage of Scripture, and I held on to the Word.

God seemed to have penned it just for me, and I trusted Him to do what His Word said He would do. This Scripture became my "stake in the ground."

God communicated through this passage His plans for our situation, and I believed Him. I knew He had given me that Scripture as a comfort and bedrock promise of what He planned to do on our behalf. A boldness rose in my heart, and I made many copies of those pages right out of the Bible I read them from. I mailed them to each business partner and expressed my belief that God was going to do just what that Scripture said. I shared this with my family, friends, church, and anyone who would listen, and told them exactly what God had given me—His Word to hang on to, and hang on I did. With all my heart I believed God.

One year later the case settled favorably.

Although no physical "David" slew our giant, God's mighty and creative hands "brought the enemy down...their feet were tangled in the snare they set for our destruction" (Psalm 9:15-16, MSG) and "their names were erased from the roster of players" (Psalm 9:5-6, MSG). It was awesome to see those words become reality, absolutely awesome!

The attempt of the big corporation to eliminate our little company from competing in their business arena was quashed by God Himself! This has been the most important life lesson I have experienced to date, and I learned, beyond a shadow of a doubt, God means what He says. We can believe Him!

～⁊◦๛

In my research on slavery and the Underground Railroad, the irony of slave auctions conducted on courthouse steps struck an indignant chord in my spirit. The irony of one human being owned and sold to another, in chains, in front of the courthouse delivered a condemning blow on pre-Civil War justice. Of all places to hold slave auctions, why were courthouse steps so often chosen? Wasn't the courthouse the symbol of due process and equity—the place of righteous judgments by honorable men who upheld laws of decency and civility?

The Courthouse Steps quilt pattern is said to represent slaves escaping to Canada by way of the Ohio River. Ohio legislation outlawed the owning of slaves and became a symbol to refugees of freedom and justice. The pattern is a variation of the Log Cabin in which fabrics are stacked in four piles around a center block. Two stacks of dark logs and two stacks of light logs separate the blocks into groupings of light fabric and then two dark, and the blocks, customarily, are sewn into a diamond pattern.

Carol's story of injustice suffered through the abuse of the legal system, brought the Courthouse Steps pattern to mind. As the Ohio River symbolized freedom to escaping slaves, God's Word gave Carol a focus point during her time of oppression, as well.

We all face our own giants, but God's Word provides wisdom, guidance and hope for every situation. It is amazing to me how God so many times, faithfully, sweetly directs me to just the right passage I need to read or just the right person to give me the counsel I need to hear.

I love Carol's sausage factory analogy. But beyond the legal system, sometimes life itself is like a sausage factory, grinding up who-knows-what into conglomerations we are supposed to swallow. God has a word for that, too. Mark 16:18 says "and if they drink any deadly thing, it shall not hurt them." We can be at peace, even when we do not like or trust the things life forces us to digest. It is not what goes into a man that defiles him. More important than what we "eat or drink" are the things we offer to the world around us. Carol used her time of trial to offer hope and faith to everyone who listened, and she continues to do it by sharing her story with us now. Thanks, Carol!

CHAPTER 18
UNDERGROUND RAILROAD

Dustin-Lee Casey – Lincoln, Nebraska

Memories flooded in as I struggled to focus on my teacher enthusiastically expounding on the benefits of good writing skills. In the dimly lit classroom of the local Christian college, his simple words, "Write a paper on a childhood memory," dredged up feelings of dread and despair.

Although my childhood had many wonderful, happy moments, a few terrible experiences still haunted me. Oblivious to my classmates, the room began to swarm with long constrained memories tumbling from the past into the here and now. The image of my teacher blurred to the moment my innocence was ripped away. I pushed the horrible memory out of my head. "Be strong," I told myself.

My thoughts jumped from the first unwelcome recollection to a junior high confrontation with bullies and punks. They taunted me and called me names, and then hit me. I turned my head to dispel the scene from my mind.

I realized I must have a terrible look on my face when the person seated next to me asked if something was wrong. "Just swallowed some sour gum," I said, trying to pull myself together, but I knew my words did not hide the terror in my eyes.

I attempted to reconnect with the teacher who continued lecturing at the front of the room, but when I looked his direction, in my mind, I was suddenly seated in my grandparents' living room. We were watching late night television, and with this memory, I felt a measure of peace.

I smiled thinking about the time Grandma and I attempted to get Grandpa from the house to the car. We wheeled him to the porch and looked at each other wondering how in the world we were going to him down the steps. Overweight and the recipient of dual hip and knee replacements, Grandpa could barely walk. Carefully, we worked together clearing the first step, then the second. With just two more to go, the wheelchair slipped. Grandpa still on board the chair, bounced down one step and then the other. Grandma and I frantically attempted to get the chair back in control, but it hit the sidewalk. His weight was too much for us. Grandpa tipped backward, and thankfully, we were able to ease him gently to the ground.

Grandma and I were horrified, but when we looked at Grandpa, he was grinning from ear to ear. "Well… Is there a plan B?" he asked and we all laughed.

I recalled Grandma's constant admonition, then. "That's what you have to do," she would say. "You have to either laugh or you are going to cry."

The faded and another came to mind. It was another time in my grandparents' kitchen. I was helping clean for an upcoming holiday while Great Aunt Lou unloaded the dishwasher. Although Aunt Lou suffered with Alzheimer's, Grandma often gave her simple tasks to occupy her time and make her feel needed.

Aunt Lou was looking puzzled at something she pulled from the dishwasher, and I walked over to see if she needed help. What I thought was a utensil turned out to be the kitchen TV's silver remote control. Aunt Lou had loaded it and run it through the dishwasher. Grandma and I looked at each other and laughed. That was the first time she whispered in my ear, "You just have to laugh or you're going to cry."

Leaving the memory of the kitchen, I suddenly recalled standing in the living room with my cousin Nikki. I loved Nikki and considered her the sister I never had. "You don't belong here, Dustin," she said. Her words cut like a knife. "Grandma and Grandpa don't need to take care of a 16-year-old."

That comment touched off a family feud. Though I never participated in the conflict, it centered on me and involved other complicated family matters. It broke my heart to watch some of my closest relatives fight so aggressively over things so insignificant.

The procession of memories continued and next I recalled a dark, cold February night. I was sitting in my car. The radio pumped in music, but I was not really listening, just sitting in the dark letting the beat pulse through me. Only an hour before, I had said goodbye to my grandfather who had passed away. A warm blanket of calm wrapped around me. Grandma opened the passenger door and slipped into the passenger seat. I turned the volume down and began the drive home.

"I can't explain it, Grandma," I attempted to describe my feelings. "I just know everything is going to be okay. I feel like God is telling me that—that everything is going to be ok."

Grandma smiled. "I feel that blanket of calm, too, Dustin, and I feel God telling me the same thing. It's all going to be okay." We looked at each other and smiled, and continued to make our way back to the house.

The memories fell away and I focused once more on my teacher still rambling on about writing, as enthusiastically as ever. Exhausted from the roller coaster ride, I wanted to run—run away from all the emotions flooding my system, but I could not move.

In my paralysis, I felt that familiar blanket of calm wrap around my spirit and a peaceful voice whisper, "Look at all the good God has brought from all the bad." I realized then, that God had always watched over me, and I noticed the little markers along the way. I saw His hand working in my life from the very beginning.

Because of severe bullying, I had been moved to a Christian school where I fell in love with God. From the Christian school I was able to home school, which allowed me to move in with my grandparents. I learned many life lessons helping Grandma take care of Grandpa and Great Aunt Lou, and I matured over the year and a half I lived with them. After my time there, I was able to move on and deal with the affects of childhood abuse.

I realized that through all the difficult moments, God led me to this seat, this day, in this Christian college where I am now pursuing a career in youth ministry. I have a passion to help kids who are dealing with some of the same things I experienced and share the healing touch of Jesus with them. There's no need to fear when God is on your side. "Don't be afraid, for I am with you. Don't be discouraged,

93

for I am your God. I will strengthen you and help you. I will hold you up with my victorious right hand (Isaiah 41:10, NLT)."

The Underground Railroad quilt pattern is a traditional block with alternating paths of dark and light. Made of a combination of four-patch and half square triangle units, simple piecing methods are utilized to assemble the complex design. Blocks sewn together, side by side, create diagonal pathways that cross the quilt top. Also known as Jacob's Ladder and Stepping Stones, each of the unique pattern names share a common element of "going somewhere."

Suggestions have been made that the Underground Railroad pattern revealed which way escaping slaves should travel. Direction indicated by the angle in which this quilt was displayed outside the home of an abolitionist may have marked safe routes on the journey to freedom.

As I read Dustin's story, his shifting memories leading from one place to the next reminded me of the steps on an Underground Railroad quilt pattern. Dustin's life experiences seemed to unfold haphazardly, like the wooden blocks of a Jacob's ladder folk toy cascading down ribbons or strings in a vibrant optical illusion.

Looking back, Dustin discovered for himself that what seemed haphazard—what appeared to be a path leading to nowhere—in truth was paved with stepping stones that would prepare him for a lifetime of ministry to others. No one enjoys suffering, but often life's lessons are most succinct when learned in life's pains. Our difficulties mark the routes of our individual pathways to freedom. Along the way, dark pieces and light work together to reveal the path of our lives—a path we walk without fear knowing God is with us and He holds us with His victorious right hand.

CHAPTER 19
INDEPENDENCE SQUARE

LauraLee Shaw - Plano, Texas

Her name was Gloria, and she was like no other. Those who knew her when she was young said she was gorgeous—a freckled, red-haired firecracker—a total knockout and full of life. Not long after her marriage and the birth of her first child, a missed stoplight turned Gloria's life tragically upside down. On her way to the store to pick up some milk, a semi flattened her car. She was not wearing her seatbelt and the impact threw her into the backseat.

Gloria sustained terrible head and upper body injuries. Her legs were pinned under the driver's seat, and she was pronounced dead at the scene. But against the odds, paramedics revived her and rushed her to a nearby emergency room. After seeing the damage to her brain and internal organs, doctors made dire predictions. They believed she would not survive the trauma and if she did, she would be in a vegetative state. At the very best, they said she would be severely handicapped with little use of her legs or arms.

But Gloria paid no mind to their predictions. After three months in a coma and several more months in ICU, against the odds, she determined to live. She endured intense physical therapy and with prayer and support from family and friends, she re-learned how to crawl and then walk, to cope and talk. Gloria returned home, and after a few years, gave birth to a second child—a miracle baby, the newspaper called her.

If the story ended there, we could read it with cheerful inspiration, but it did not—not by far. Gloria's days were filled with struggles.

With everything in her, she fought to do the things most of us take for granted. Her spine and one of her arms, permanently bent, left her with a crippled gate. Extensive damage to her voice box left her voice low, loud and raspy. Children and strangers often stared. The damage to her legs made her unsteady on her feet for the remainder of her life, while brain trauma impaired her mental state and emotional maturity.

Gloria's husband struggled to know and love her in this new way, but turned to alcohol to deal with his own handicaps. With the drink, he began abusing Gloria physically and emotionally. After several years, and with the new realization her daughters were also being abused, Gloria filed for divorce. Her financial support gone, she struggled again to learn to function, this time as a single mother.

Daily plagued with severe headaches, physical pain and emotional insecurity, Gloria endeavored to raise two young children on disability and public aid. Her mother, sisters and local church helped her and her daughters maneuver through school and life. She coped as best she could and the same tenaciousness, ornery spirit from her youth kept her going in spite of her adversities.

She lived as independently as possible, driving her kids to school and extra curricular activities. She made pot roasts and sheet cakes and exercised on a stationery bike to keep her muscles as strong as possible. In their small town, people enjoyed Gloria's sense of humor and dramatic perspective on life. She lived somewhere in the middle of child and adult—communicating like an adult, but thinking and responding to situations more like a nine- or ten-year-old.

The years saw Gloria in and out of the hospital. She suffered various illnesses, survived a series of car accidents, wove through delusional and paranoid behaviors and tried to cope with an empty house when her daughters went off to college. Every day she took numerous medications, each one fixing a different symptom or problem diagnosed by one of her several doctors. She chose to live alone and "take care of herself." The consequences, incredible loneliness and fear, were wrapped in the satisfaction of making it on her own.

Gloria's sister, pastor and church family helped make her desire to live independently a reality. They sacrificially attended her needs, allowing her to maintain her dignity as much as possible. Though both her daughters tried to persuade Gloria to live with them, she felt comfortable with her life the way it was.

September 11, 2006, after a month of struggling in ICU to recover from a simple procedure, Gloria's battles came to an end. The list of lessons we could learn from her life is long, at least it is for me. Gloria was my mother and I am her miracle baby.

As a child, I saw my mother as abnormal and somewhat embarrassing. As a young adult, she was an obligation and sometimes a nuisance. Now, looking back on her life after she has gone—well, I have a new perspective.

Somehow, over time, the memories of her crinkled forehead while she moaned in pain and discomfort are replaced with the memory of Mom on her knees praying by her bed at night. Instead of recalling her smoking cigarette after cigarette, I remember with incredible admiration how she decided to quit one day and never smoked again. All the embarrassing comments she made, along with the neediness that drained me dry at times, are secondary to the vivid memories of her sitting at the table reading the wrinkled, coffee-stained pages of her Bible. When I'm tempted to focus on the memories of her fits of paranoia, the Lord faithfully reminds me of the verses of Scripture she clung to and quoted during the last days of her life in ICU.

I've often wished I could ask God face-to-face why He allowed my mom to suffer so long, so hard and so deep, but I know that my mind could not understand even if He told me. So instead of questioning, I choose to be thankful—for one Scriptural nugget in particular that reminds me of what made Mom's life valuable to all who knew her.

"But God chose the foolish things of the world to shame the wise. He chose the weak things of the world to shame the strong. God chose the things of this world that are common and looked down on. He chose what is not considered to be important to do away with what is considered to be important. So no one can brag to God" (1 Corinthians 1:27-29, NIRV).

Life with Mom taught me that true strength comes from God, and it is magnified when I am weak. Although "wrecks" in life are inevitable, with God, we can overcome the challenges they bring.

The Independence Square pattern, although not part of the "Quilt Code," is a modern-day symbol of freedom. Philadelphia's Independence Square, the site of the signing of the Declaration of Independence, is known as the birthplace of our nation. Although it is true that at our nation's inception the Constitution allowed slavery as a legal practice, it is also true we have grown from that time. Youth often acts impetuously, thus the admonition in Scripture to "flee youthful lusts." As our nation matured, it paid a great price to right this great wrong, and regardless of political persuasion, the recent election of our first black president testifies to how far we have come on the issue of equality for all races.

As listed in the <u>Encyclopedia of Pieced Quilt Patterns</u>, the Independence Square has been created in two variations, most commonly, a simple "equal nine-patch," but also an "unequal pieced nine-patch," the difference being a large center square in the "unequal" pattern that throws off the uniform lines of its forerunner. Life is like that for some…unequal in its demands, thrown off course by the unexpected. It doesn't seem fair Gloria faced so many difficulties…challenges that rippled into the lives of her family and friends. But when she persevered and accepted help from others and God, although her life "pattern" skewed from what most experience as normal, it was still a pattern of independence that brought glory to God. And that's what her name means: glory!

While I don't claim to be a great theologian or philosopher, it seems true independence comes when we realize we are truly dependent. "No man is an island" proclaims the cliché—a truth that became a truism because it is so true. True freedom comes when we freely choose to give our lives to God. True spiritual strength abounds when we first realize our human limitations and learn to trust God to make up the difference.

CHAPTER 20
DRESDEN PLATE

Lynnette Countaway - Paw Paw, Michigan

It had been a hard day at work. Exhausted, I stepped through the front door and threw my keys and purse on the entryway table. A sigh slipped out as I walked into the kitchen and pulled a drink out of the refrigerator. I began to unwind as I slowly sipped the cool drink.

I reached a hand back unconsciously and began kneading the tense areas in my shoulders and the side of my neck. "Wow, I sure am sore today," I thought. I took another sip and glanced out the back window at the hot tub. "A good soak will loosen me up."

My work as a dental hygienist had begun to take its toll on my body. Over the last ten years, my neck and shoulders, as well as my lower back, were all taking the brunt of the physical stress of my job.

I changed my clothes, climbed into the hot tub and gradually began to relax as bubbling jets sent warm water swirling around me. The tension of the day eased. I leaned back, dropped my shoulders beneath the water and gazed up in wonder at the beautiful Catskill Mountains.

From my house, built at the base of the mountain range, I had a remarkable view. The splendor of God's creation spread out before me in a breathtaking panorama. Signs of the season dotted the landscape—trees just beginning to turn brilliant reds, yellows and oranges. Crickets lifted their twilight songs as the comfortably warm afternoon faded into early evening. A gentle breeze blew over my skin and I took a deep breath, inhaling the sweet earthen smell of fall and realizing how very rich God's blessings were in my life.

I sent up silent thanks and praise thinking about how good God had been to give my husband and me this home, our first home, in this lovely area of New York. Just recently married, becoming a pastor's wife, and then moving from my home state hundreds of miles away brought many new challenges to my life and faith. Leaving my loved ones, my church and all that was familiar to me had been more difficult than I had imagined.

I was homesick. Over the year we had lived in New York I returned to Michigan a couple of times to see my family and friends. The visits helped me cope with the transition, but other factors sometimes overwhelmed me. In addition to all the changes and the new responsibilities of assisting my husband, I also started a new job at the local hospital in the dental residency program.

As I continued to soak in the warm tub, relaxing and enjoying the pastoral view, I began talking to God. I poured out my heart and told Him all the things I felt about my day and my thoughts on being so homesick. I felt Him with me and my heart filled with gratitude for all His blessings. I couldn't hold it in any more. "God, I love you so much!" I said aloud. "You have been so good to me."

The interlude was so sweet, just a calm conversation with no Holy Ghost "goose bumps" or tears—just God and me chatting in the hot tub.

The next day was routine. When I came home from work, I puttered around the house until I heard a knock on my door. I opened it, and there stood one of the saints in our church, Sister Donna. She was carrying a vase of long-stemmed red roses, a full dozen of them. "Come in," I said, holding the door for her.

She walked inside and set the vase on the table. "Today a patient gave these to me and the Lord spoke to me and told me: Take these to Sister Countaway. So, here I am!"

Immediately the Lord reminded me of our time together the night before. In my spirit I heard Him whisper, "I love you, too."

My eyes filled with tears as I realized my precious Jesus used this sweet sister to send me a dozen of my favorite flowers. Red roses, the symbol of love, showed me God really loved me and He wanted to let me know He had heard every word I said the night before.

What a wonderful and awesome God. He cared enough to take the time to send flowers to one of His daughters. The Lord knew I was overwhelmed with all the changes and new responsibilities in my life and He sent a special delivery message, a beautiful bouquet He knew would be just the little "pick me up" I needed. Through this simple act, I felt so loved and my spirit encouraged and strengthened to press on.

❧❧❧

Although the Dresden Plate quilt pattern was not part of the "Quilt code," Dresden was a known stop and destination on the Underground Railroad. The historic site of the actual Uncle Tom's Cabin, made famous through the writings of Harriet Beecher Stowe, is located in the village of Dresden, Ontario. The book, Uncle Tom's Cabin, credited as being a vital antislavery tool, was originally published as a 40-week serial in an abolitionist paper. Published in book form in 1852, the work gained such popularity during the 19th Century it was second in distribution only to the Bible.

The Dresden cabin commemorates the life of Rev. Josiah Henson who became famous after Harriet Beecher Stowe acknowledged his life experiences as the source for her fictional character, Uncle Tom. A slave for 41 years, Rev. Henson and his family escaped and moved to Dresden where he founded the Dawn Settlement, a refuge and place of new beginning for escaped slaves.

Built in 1856 by abolitionist George Willison Adams, Prospect Place, a 29-room mansion just north of Dresden, Ohio, is also a confirmed station along the Underground Railroad.

The roots of the Dresden Plate quilt block have been linked to a china pattern in far away Dresden, Germany. The blocks are made with fabric appliquéd in a round of radiating flat-sided "petals," usually from a central circle that looks more like a flower than a plate.

Speaking of plates, Lynnette's was certainly full with all the changes she faced as life's twists and turns took their toll. But what a sweet encounter she shared with the Lord in the quiet of her day.

The beautiful gift of flowers she received, reminds us all that God cares—God is listening—and He is loving us all back in His own special way.

CHAPTER 21
CROSSING OHIO

Don Wisler – Dublin, Ohio

I like to ride my bike. Not the leisurely ride around the neighborhood, but rather, I like to head out for 20 to 25 miles from home (the direction doesn't really matter), and then find my way home.

In the summer of 2008, I took an extended trip and rode across Ohio, starting in Kentucky, crossing the Ohio River, and ending up in Sandusky, where I dipped my wheel into Lake Erie. From start to finish on this week-long ride with 300 other cyclists, I pedaled about 450 miles. That would have been enjoyable enough, but what made the trip even more memorable was that we visited many of the stops along the old routes of the Underground Railroad.

Along the way, I discovered there are many things to learn riding a bike. You might think that with so many people on the ride we traveled in large groups. With different skill levels and no set departing time, I actually spent a lot of time riding by myself. I ride without an iPod or other "noisemaker," preferring instead to enjoy the outdoors and be with my own thoughts. When I quieted myself, I opened myself to prayer. I couldn't help but pray.

I did not simply hop on a bike and ride 450 miles. A lot of preparation and practice came beforehand. To be good at anything, you have to prepare and practice. The more I ride, the stronger I am at cycling. We get good at what we practice—good skills and habits as well as bad. It might be riding a bike, learning new things, developing relationship skills, or watching TV, eating too much of the wrong things, being an inattentive spouse or not spending time being the best parent possible. We get good at the things we spend time doing. I learned to ask myself, "Am I practicing the things I need to get good at? Are the things I am practicing helping me to achieve my goals or to become the kind of person I want to be? Or am I working against myself by practicing the wrong things?"

Some rides are easier than others, but no worthwhile ride is easy all the way. To think otherwise only invites frustration. It helps to prepare for challenges along the way. When I first started riding, I often looked only for the tailwinds and backed away from the tougher hills. While I would rather ride with the wind at my back on a downhill slope, I have come to realize that the easy rides do not make me a better cyclist. To improve, I must challenge myself and sometimes try things I might prefer to avoid. I do not mind the wind now. I even look forward to a nice series of rolling hills. They make me stronger.

I found that if I charge into a hill, it often is a bit easier than I anticipated. So I try to ask myself, "Where in my life am I backing away from the challenges or avoiding the things I find difficult?" I do not necessarily go out of my way to ride into the wind or go up a long hill, but if they are there, I try to embrace them and take them head on.

Equipment is important. You have to take care of your bike. It is not necessary to have the most expensive bike or the one with the most gears. Every rider finished the ride, whether they had 30 gears or just 3. But those who cared well for their equipment had fewer problems along the way. Every morning, I made sure to properly inflate the tires, clean and lube the chain and check the brakes.

Proper clothes help prevent blisters and sores. The helmet is especially important. I know a few guys who have been told that, had they not been wearing their helmet, a crash would have likely killed them.

In addition to caring for my equipment, I also had to care for myself. It was important to stay hydrated, keep electrolyte levels in good balance, and take proper nutrition regularly – before thirst and hunger set in. Otherwise, I could have found myself in a lot of trouble fast. A few riders had to drop out because they did not properly tend to these basic needs.

Reflecting on this during the ride, I wondered, "How am I caring for myself and those who are important to me? What preventative maintenance do I need to help me avoid equipment failure down the road? How do I nurture myself physically? Emotionally? Intellectually? Relationally? Spiritually? How do I nurture those I love?" I need to do this before I'm running on empty.

While I was alone for much of the ride, there were a number of opportunities to ride with small groups. Those not involved in cycling may not realize how much of a "team" sport it really is. Riding with others always provides a bit of encouragement, but there are many other advantages to riding in a group or peloton. You may have seen cyclists riding in a line with only a few feet or inches between wheels, rather than shoulder to shoulder. When riding in a "pace" line, a tremendous drafting effect takes place. Riders behind the front rider almost get pulled along. Studies have shown their effort to maintain the same speed is reduced by 25 to 35 percent!

In life, it is important to connect with those who are headed in the same direction. It makes doing the right thing easier. Although you have to take your turn leading or pulling others, you do not have to go it alone all the time. You are able to get farther and reach your goals faster when cooperating and working together with like-minded people.

Again, I have to regularly examine my life choices. "Am I choosing to associate with the right people, or am I just 'along for the ride,' going wherever they lead?" If I am just along for the ride, I may end up somewhere I do not want to go. For me, I find that church serves as a necessary and helpful peloton on our Christian journey.

While it might be an overused cliché, the road along the way can be just as important as reaching the destination. It often feels so good to get off the saddle at the end of a ride, but there can be a bit of a let-down, even at the end of a long, tough ride. I am learning to pay attention to the things along the way.

I saw a lot of wildlife crossing Ohio roads or out in the fields as I went by. Of course, I kept my eye on the road ahead, but there was plenty of opportunity to look around. When I took the time to be aware of the warmth of the sun, the cool breeze, the clouds in the sky and the sights and sounds around me, rather than just working hard at getting finished, things seemed to flow. It actually became a spiritual experience. Life is a lot like riding a bike. Take care of your bike, start pedaling and enjoy the ride!

　　　　　　　　　　　♡✂♡

The Crossing Ohio quilt pattern appears to be a derivative of the Ohio Star block. Mini squares form a bold X across an Ohio Star, and "X marks the spot." Although a more contemporary pattern, not dated to the antebellum era, the act of Crossing Ohio was indeed an integral part of the journey to freedom for so many.

A good number of the routes of the Underground Railroad avoided cities and settlements with larger populations. More people meant a greater risk of being seen, which meant a greater risk of being caught. Refugees often traveled across farmlands and woods, keeping to themselves until they came upon safe places to stop along the way.

The Crossing Ohio pattern connects to the flight of runaway slaves at the location of Paynes Crossing in rural Ohio. This community eventually became a free African American settlement. Along with others in the area, this settlement appears to have served as a major station on the Underground Railroad in the years prior to and during the Civil War.

Don's Ohio crossing, unique in its tracing of the Underground Railroad through the state, gives a wonderful illustration of the many ways God speaks to us through our environment and circumstances. Every question he asked himself along the way and after, I examined in my own heart and mind.

Don's physically challenging journey brought many rewards. While his body labored, the mind and spirit enthralled in the wonder and beauty of God. Following the route of the "railroad" turned trail, paths and country roads, he cycled his way amid the landscape of rolling farmlands, towns, and forests accompanied by songbirds, musings and prayers.

I feel peaceful just thinking about it. Although I know I would poop out after the first few miles, the sanctuary of his bicycle seat seems a wonderful place to commune with God and enjoy the world He made. I can be so driven, consumed with the tasks at hand and thinking only to the end of a project or season. Thank you, Don, for sharing your story, and encouraging me to remember to not only prepare for the journey, but enjoy it, as well—a liberating way to think and live!

"When we walk to the edge of all the light we have and take a step into the darkness of the unknown, we must believe one of two things will happen·there will be something solid for us to stand upon, or we will be taught to fly"
– Anonymous

CHAPTER 22
TUMBLING BLOCKS

Chris Gueydan – Raymond, Mississippi

In the midst of immense beauty, a secret killer hides. Four years ago, my wife and I took our sons to the Grand Canyon. We camped several nights on the South Rim. The terrain is rugged and intense, and the Canyon's dangers very real. Every year, nearly 250 people die in the Canyon. Most get too close to the edge of the cliffs, and either the edge gives way or they fall off.

When I stood with my family on the rim and looked down to the bottom 5,000 feet below, it appeared to be an easy descent. We watched hikers move down the Canyon, and it seemed the trek would take only a few hours. The grade was inviting—downhill all the way— and it looked like we could trot easily for hours with little strain.

What we can't know from looking is that the temperature at the bottom of the trail and in the belly of the Canyon is 30 to 40 degrees hotter than at the top, and the trail that looks so manageable is a full 13 miles long. Many conscientious hikers begin their journeys with a bottle of water, but soon find one bottle is not enough to prevent dehydration in the intense heat; and dehydration kills.

During our campout, my family and I enjoyed our time on the trails, but were careful to avoided overdoing on our Canyon hikes. Before starting out, we loaded our backpacks with several liters of water, jerky and granola bars. We enjoyed our hikes, emerging from each one safely. After several great days, we broke camp and loaded up the car content. On the drive home, we soon discovered we were far from "home free." Another danger—also hidden to the eye—lay ahead.

Our trip began well. We stopped in Amarillo at the Big Texan, a restaurant famous for their 72 ounce steaks—larger than most roasts. Our ten-year-old son placed his order, but when the food came, he said he felt sick before his first bite. He complained of feeling cold and went outside to lay down on a porch swing.

His brothers took turns going outside to check on him. My wife and I thought he might be coming down with something, maybe a virus, but when we checked on him, he lay shivering on the swing in 100° Fahrenheit temperatures.

My wife Donya, a nursing student at the time, knew this was very unusual, and she called a classmate to get her advice. Thank God her friend was home. She compiled a list of signs and symptoms and checked the internet for medical information, reporting back to us what she found. All he said was, "I don't feel good," but early on Donya thought he might have appendicitis. She pressed down on his abdomen and then quickly let go, but he had no pain when his abdominal wall rebounded from the test, one of the "sure-fire" textbook signs of appendicitis.

We traveled on, and over the next hundred miles my wife constantly reassessed his condition. As we entered Childress, Texas, Donya was convinced. "This is appendicitis," she said. Somehow, after all those miles, just at the moment she said it, I believed it, too. I looked up and immediately saw a blue "H" sign and followed it to the Emergency Room entrance at Childress Hospital.

During the admissions process Donya told the ER personnel she thought the problem was his appendix. "We don't have a regular surgeon here," the hospital clerk said. "We can fly you to Dallas, and that will take a few hours." Within just a few minutes of our entrance, before arrangements could be made, a surgeon arrived. He was not on staff at Childress Hospital but periodically drove in from out of state when needed and was scheduled to perform a gallbladder surgery. He heard about my son and said he would either make sure he got to Dallas, or he would perform the surgery as soon as the operating room was free. Everything worked in our favor. The doctor completed a successful operation, and two days later we finished our journey home to Raymond, Mississippi.

When I look back at everything that happened: surviving 100 degree temperatures in the Grand Canyon, a sick little boy burning with fever in the panhandle of Texas, looking up to find an "H" sign just when we determined to go to the hospital, then a surgeon arriving just when we needed him…

When I look at all these things, I wonder just what are the chances of all of this being "just chance?" I don't believe it was all coincidence. I believe it was all a miracle—including the fact that my wife's nursing school friend was home near her computer.

But there is more yet. As we began receiving bills for all the accrued medical expenses, we were informed our medical insurance did not cover out-of-state surgeries. Thankfully, the Lord saw fit to take care of our outstanding debt for this hospitalization; a bill, that for two college students, seemed as deep as the Grand Canyon.

So my miracle happened, and miracles will happen—do happen every day. It is my desire that sharing this story will encourage people to remember that although the path can be long, up and down, and at times painful, when our hearts and minds are open to God, we can make it through. And the Lord who made the Grand Canyon, and appendices, and doctors, and smart nursing students, and children, and all of us, will make a way when we need Him. With our faith in Him, we are free from worry as God orders the steps and circumstances of our days.

⟿ ⟾

One glance at a Tumbling Blocks quilt, and the illusion of movement compels a second look. The pattern, one of many that represents home life, is a one-patch quilt design made of single, repeating shapes. The arrangement of light, medium, and dark patches creates the illusion of tumbling blocks, and the pattern is first recorded as used by Victorian ladies to show off scraps of their finest silk fabrics.

As recorded in *Hidden in Plain View*, Ozella Wilson said a Tumbling Blocks quilt on display was a sign to "gather food, clothing, and anything that could be used as weapons." It was a symbol indicating it was time for slaves to pack up and go, that a conductor was in the area to see them aboard the Underground Railroad.

Miss Wilson said the pattern was also a code name for Niagara Falls, a landmark for escaping slaves indicating they had arrived at the Canadian border. Although the likelihood of refugees swimming across the rapid waters is slim, it is possible a ferry below the falls or a footbridge available at the time were used. History records Harriet Tubman used a railroad bridge built in 1855 to transport passengers across the river by train.

Elements in Chris's story relate to the Tumbling Blocks pattern in several ways—beginning with the possibility of tumbling down the Grand Canyon. Secondly, the pattern is said to represent a well known natural wonder, Niagara Falls, and the magnificent Canyon is a natural wonder, as well. But more than the physical elements, the way the pieces of Chris' story connected and fell into place brought this pattern to mind. Reflecting back on the details of the trip, the Gueyden family recognized the miraculous way everything played out, even the difficult aspects, and that gave them a new assurance God was in control and ordering their steps. He brought them to a place of safety and provided all their needs. To me, the Tumbling Blocks pattern looks somewhat like a set of steps, as well. Thank God for the freedom from worry we experience when we trust God to order our steps.

Chapter 23
Cats and Mice

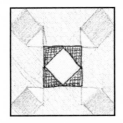

Maria Spencer — Poland, Ohio

Dandelions popping up in the Spring don't bother me—not now, anyway. Tackling endless yard work, rising mounds of laundry and dust bunnies reproducing in my house were once at the top of my to-do lists. I worried over clothes on the floor. I fretted if the kitchen was not stocked with special snacks for my family. If the house looked less than great, I carried anxiety about that, too. I worked a full-time job, but somehow felt if I was not fussing over the daily household chores, I was not a good wife and mom.

Constant, consistent worry filled my days. I learned at a very young age the amount of love you have for someone equals the amount of time you spend outwardly worrying about them, or so I thought. My outlook and priorities changed in one quick moment.

On the day of my three-month-old daughter's traditional baptism, Olivia came down with a high fever. Confident of a simple diagnosis, my husband and I took her to the pediatric emergency room for an examination. We expected to receive a prescription for an antibiotic and go home, but we were quite wrong.

After drawing every type of fluid from her tiny body, the physician said Olivia had a very high white blood cell count and they needed to determine why. As the nurse prepared a needle to start an antibiotic, Olivia stopped breathing. Right in front of my eyes, her glowing pink skin turned varying shades of gray.

An alarm rang throughout the hospital. The trauma team raced to action. I'll never forget the sights and sounds during those moments, and though the crisis was great, I did not pray.

When Olivia stabilized, we were allowed to see her. The tiny, 11-pound baby girl who began her day in a long, white baptismal gown, was now connected to many wires, each leading to different pieces of medical equipment. We felt like we stepped into the middle of a horrible nightmare.

I now had something very real to worry about. Every priority shifted. In a very short period of time I realized with dismay I never spent any time in prayer. I had no point of reference for a spiritual life, or how to even begin a conversation with God, and I knew the medical crisis with Olivia was so great I could not handle it in my own strength.

When we finally brought Olivia home, grateful for her life, we thanked God for guiding our steps to the emergency room that night. Had we put her to bed, she would have died in her sleep.

Three months after Olivia's hospital stay, we realized she was not opening her left hand as she should, nor was she lifting her left leg and foot. Brain trauma suffered during her illness had left her with hemiplegic cerebral palsy.

I spent the first year and a half trying to make sense of everything that happened. "Why her? Why us?" I wondered. I focused most of my attention on her limitations, neglecting to notice her strengths. A deep depression settled in, one I thought I would never recover from. I reasoned that if I accepted this disability, and did not outwardly show the world how much pain and worry it caused, I was a bad Mom. How could I love my beautiful daughter and not be constantly worried about her health and welfare?

Through the pain, God used Olivia to bring me into a personal relationship with Him. As she drew strength from me, I sought strength from God. There was no other option; in order to get out of my ashes and care for my daughter, I had to cling to His promises and His hope. I accepted Jesus as my Lord and Savior, and held on to His Word: "…(the Lord will) provide for those who grieve in Zion-to bestow on them a crown of beauty instead of ashes, the oil of gladness instead of mourning, and a garment of praise instead of a spirit of despair"(Isaiah 61:7, NIV).

Prior to the trauma, I was a supervisor at our local Early Intervention program, and when I returned from leave, I began a new position as parent-to-parent staff. For the past four years, I have helped families with children of a variety of delays and disabilities as a Family Support Specialist.

Through my experiences, I felt the Lord direct me to write for other "special" parents. I now write a monthly column for our local Parent magazine entitled, "Special Parents, Special Kids." The column, though not directly related to a ministry or church, provides a platform to offer parents hope for their children's futures.

It is both humbling and overwhelming to look back and see how God turned the most painful days of my life into such beauty— that His love can be seen and heard through my words and my daughter's life. Olivia is six years old and doing great. She wears braces on both legs to help her balance to walk. A testimony to God's goodness, Olivia is full of light and joy. She draws comments from strangers on her beautiful spirit, a living example of John 9:2 (NIV). "His disciples asked 'who sinned, this man or his parents, that he was born blind?' 'Neither this man nor his parents sinned,' said Jesus, 'but this happened so that the work of God might be displayed in his life.'"

When Spring rolls around each year, and my neighbors probably cringe at the sight of the dandelions in my yard, I smile and thank the Lord He showed my husband and me a great lesson. The little things that bother so many people are really not important.

Olivia sees dandelions as pretty yellow flowers to pick for her mommy—bright creations from God, as is she. My priorities have forever changed and my mission is no longer to be the best gardener or housekeeper, but to be the best mom I can be to Olivia and her brother, Jonah. God has given me a passion to help special parents everywhere realize they were chosen by Him to parent their children—and know that with the help of God, they don't have to live a life of worry. They can stop and enjoy the dandelions, too.

Hired men chased down runaway slaves using every means at their disposal. Though not a "Quilt Code" pattern, the Cats and Mice quilt design reminded me of the hunt and chase, man hunting man during the slave era. The pattern, a nine-X design, uses small triangles of varying colors to make square patches that connect to the sides of a solid center square. Attached to these four multi-colored squares, matching solid squares elongate the X to the corners of each block. Sewn together, the busy pattern sends the eye scurrying in every direction following the lines in a colorful maze.

Maria's story also brought to mind the Cats and Mice pattern— not necessarily the circumstances surrounding her daughter's illness, but the way her thought patterns worked. I confess, I have fallen prey many times to the treadmill of unachievable perfection. I see myself as the cat, and the mice just keep reproducing and scampering about like Maria's dust bunnies—laundry, kids, husband, kids' school work, house work, volunteer work, work work, and the list goes on. Life moves so fast we can hardly keep up, especially to the unrealistic expectations we set for ourselves when we lift up our self-made goal, a Frankensteinial, perfectionistic conglomeration of *Martha Stewart Living, Better Homes & Garden, Working Mother, Christianity Today, Fit* and *Cosmopolitan*. Like Maria, I have decided to jump off the treadmill and, like a cat, land on my feet. Matthew 6:23-34 gives advice to worriers. The short version is: do not worry about your life, your clothes, your food or your body. After all, worrying will not add a single hour to our lives.

We cat-thinking, mouse-chasing people would do well to get a reality check. Statistically there will always be more mice than cats. Mice start breeding at 6 weeks of age, and their incubation period is 18-20 days. Cat breeders recommend waiting until felines are 18 months before breeding with an incubation period of 63 days. Do the math. We will always have more mice than cats. So let's just make friends.

CHAPTER 24
MORNING GLORY

Constance Gilbert – Bend, Oregon

Up from his nap, raring to go, my toddler and I headed out the door to walk off some energy. We stopped at a neighbor's house to play and chat, and when we returned home, our little dog, Brandy, was pacing and whining. She usually jumped up and down with an "I'm glad to see you" greeting, but something seemed out of sorts—a combination of a "someone's coming" bark and crying.

Brandy ran a few feet ahead and stopped. I knew she wanted me to follow, but I went in the house to let my husband know we were back from our walk. I looked in the bedroom where he was resting when we left. He was not there. I called out for him and searched through the house, but he was nowhere to be found. Then…I followed Brandy.

No one expects to be widowed at 27 years old. No one wants to believe a loving husband would intentionally leave her. Mine did. He took his life and left me alone to raise our two year-old son. In the confusion, looking for his daddy and dealing with his own pain, my son directed his anger towards me, adding to my grief and the heavy weight I carried.

The first months that followed were a blur, followed by a mix of great sorrow and whys. Eventually, numbness set in; the only way I managed to get through each day. The nights were the darkest. Nightmares reigned, even when I failed to sleep.

The Christmas holidays came, dressed in all the glitter and tradition of the season. Under the pretty wrappings, my heart broke a bit more each day with a pain so excruciating it was beyond definition. The bleakness of Winter matched my emotions and when Spring, my favorite season finally emerged, I did not even notice.

I smiled for my son, prepared meals, made beds, did laundry— all the mommy stuff life required. Family and friends remarked how well I was doing, but inside, I was distraught, magnified by the feeling that no one understood. I was not okay.

The days, the weeks, came and went. Rage simmered on low for months, but it was seething now, churning just below the surface. I had prayed, talked with friends and tried counseling, but nothing helped. Nothing filled the void. The only reason I was still alive was the precious three-year-old napping inside. He had lost a father. He should not have to lose a mother, too. But for me, being alive wasn't living. I wanted it all to end. I wanted to die.

As I walked across the back yard, anger consumed me. Nothing existed beyond the pain and loneliness. I did not notice the grass that needed mowing or my yellow rosebush with new blossoms burgeoning forth on knotty stems. The sun beamed down on my skin, but its warmth was lost to me.

With each step, the rage roiled and churned until it violently percolated, then penetrated the filter of my façade and burst into full boil. I screamed long and loud, like the persistent whistling of a teakettle no one took off the burner. With clinched fists and flowing the tears I cried out to the heavens, "Why, Lord?"

Harsh words, words I did not even know I knew ripped like rapids from my lips. All the pain, the hurt, the anger and heartache smashed against the rocks of my despair. I raised my arms and shook balled hands at the sky.

"God, Your love is a lie. Everything is Your fault. You let him bring the gun home. You didn't stop him. You took Him from me!"

I wanted to strike out at God and beat His chest. I wanted to blame someone and make them pay for my anguish…for my innocent son's losses. I paced. I ran. I shouted some more. I cussed and looked for something to hit.

Completely spent and hoarse, I finally collapsed on the ground and wished I had never been born.

I never felt myself fall. I just lay on the grass, too tired to get up. Time stood still for a while—at least it seemed to. In the nothingness of my mind there was no time. I willed myself to die.

In slow motion, tiny bits of the world began to awaken my senses. I smelled the tangy grass and the sweet fragrance of the lily-of-the valley nearby. The warmth of the sun comforted my face. Birds twittered and sang age-old arias. A butterfly brushed against my arm, and slowly, I opened my eyes.

Clouds billowed and fluttered in the azure sky like fluffy bunnies. Geese honked and changed the leader of their flying v formation. Even the leaves on the trees seemed greener than I ever noticed before, their shapes more defined.

I heard the squeak of the chains as my son's swing swayed in the gentle breeze, and then I heard another sound...a gentle laughter. It sounded like a babbling brook deep in a pristine forest, soothing. My body responded—muscles relaxed and breathing returned to normal. Silently, I lay in the grass surrounded by a laughter that reached into my spirit and filled me. I closed my eyes, drinking in what had escaped me for so long: calm.

I rested in the grass and clover, listening with wonder to the sweet laughter before I the Lord pressed these words into my spirit.

Child, do you remember that I gave you your feelings? That I already know your thoughts before you are able to express them? My love for you is everlasting. My Son felt all your pain before you were born.

My child, I can fill the void; I can take your pain; I can fill you with hope, love, and joy.

Dear child, you are precious to me. Crawl into my arms and let me rock you with the breeze, let me warm you with the sunshine, let me sing to you through birdsong. Surrender your all to me.

Connie, I have been waiting for you.

My lips uttered not a sound, but with my heart I answered, "I am Yours."

My world was filled with peace. When my eyes opened again, I saw the splendor of His creation. Birds sang out a rhapsody of love, and I knew I had just received a special touch of God's amazing grace.

The Morning Glory quilt pattern, though not part of the "Quilt Code," relates well to the endeavors of those embarking on the Underground Railroad. Many variations exist of the pattern, including appliqué, reverse appliqué and classic pieced blocks. Though different in their designs and creative methods, each block features a motif of floral trumpets.

When summer days draw to a close, and the afternoon sun slips closer to the horizon, brilliant blue morning glory petals fade, curl and die. But when morning comes and a new day dawns, dewy blooms unfurl—God's sweet mementos silently trumpet a message of hope: joy comes in the morning (Psalms 30:5).

The root meaning for the word "glory" in the Bible comes from the Hebrew word for "weight" or "heaviness." It has been my observation that the weight of suffering and trials a person carries is often directly proportional to the weight of the glory of God we see in their lives. Who would delight more in the glory of freedom than a person once enslaved? Who would understand more the joy that comes after pain—when darkness gives way to light and the glory of the morning unfolds like a blossom in the sunshine? The greater the darkness, the greater the glory of the morning!

Constance carried a tremendous heaviness, and when she finally reached the point she could bear no more, she found God speaking to her, first through nature, and then, Spirit to spirit. To some, such intimate communication with God is a foreign experience. It is my prayer that we all draw ever nearer to hear God's voice clearly and often. Though many have never experienced such a glorious personal word, the Lord speaks to all continually through His creation if we will but listen.

> The heavens keep telling the wonders of God,
> and the skies declare what he has done.
> Each day informs the following day;
> each night announces to the next.
> They don't speak a word, and there is never

the sound of a voice.
Yet their message reaches all the earth,
and it travels around the world.
(Psalms 19:1-4,CEV)

"For so is the will of God that by doing right
you may put to silence the ignorance of foolish
men. Live as free men, yet without using your
freedom as a pretext for evil ['naughtiness,'
'depravity']; but live as bond slaves of God.
Honor all men. Love the brotherhood. Fear God.
Honor the emperor[and/or President]."
— 1 Peter 2:15-17 [RSV]

CHAPTER 25
BRITCHES

Bill Wagner – Rochester Hills, Michigan

Being cold—that's what I remember most. An oil stove in the living room was the only source of heat in our three-bedroom ranch. Sometimes I was lucky enough to beat my seven siblings to a spot on the floor near it. Otherwise, I slept in a chair, a cot, or shared a bed in an unheated room where a bowl of water left overnight froze into a solid brick of ice by morning.

We were poor, dirty, and hungry—a ragtag bunch of mischievous, destructive kids who ripped shingles off the garage and zinged them across the yard for entertainment. One year we talked our parents into bb guns for Christmas. As quick as we unwrapped them, we shot ornaments off the tree. We shot out the windows in the barn and garage, my dad's car window, too.

Jamie was older than me by one year, and together we got into all sorts of predicaments. One summer we stole gun powder from our brother. We dug a hole, deposited the powder, threw in a match and ran a few yards away. When the explosion never came, we crept to the hole and peeked inside…just as the powder exploded. For six weeks our heads were wrapped like mummies and we made many trips to the doctor to have our faces peeled and re-wrapped.

Once, in the middle of the night, Jamie and I snuck to our neighbor's and filled burlap bags with potatoes we dug up from his field. We drug the heavy bags home and climbed into bed exhausted but pleased we had gotten away with our devilry. In the morning, Daddy answered the knock at the door and the questions from our neighbor. He asked if we took the potatoes, which we denied, but the trail we made from his field to our barn was so clear a blind man could follow it.

Yes, Jamie and I got into our share of trouble. We even shared the same pair of bellbottoms until, after daily wear, they finally gave out. In our late teens for cheap entertainment we roller skated several times a week. We drank and pretty much acted like fools, but with my feathered BeeGees hair billowing, tight-jean-clad legs moving in time with the disco beat under a twirling mirrored ball, I left my insecurities behind and reigned at the rink. There I caught the eye of a pretty, middle-class girl named Liz and we became an item.

Liz and I hung out at her house a lot. I will never forget the first time I ate corn on the cob with her family. I slapped a slab of butter in my palm, grabbed an ear of corn and slathered it up. When I finished, I dropped the corn on my plate, held both dripping hands palms up, looked around the table and asked, "Does anyone have a napkin?" Mouths gaped as everyone stared in silence. I have never buttered corn like that again. Some things can be relearned.

Liz and I dated for about a year before I finally, reluctantly invited her to my house. She thought I was ashamed of her. I was ashamed… but not of her. Approximately fifty cats and four dogs lived in our home. The day of her visit, my birthday, one of my brothers threw a cat across the table over her head. Afterwards, Mom carried the birthday cake to the table, cursing the cats and smoothing a string of paw prints out of the frosting. Liz politely refused the slice Mom offered.

As my relationship developed with Liz, Jamie and I spent less time together. There was no tension between us, we just went our separate ways. During this time, something happened that changed Jamie's life. He got saved. For years Jamie told me about God. I always had a love for God, and I was happy for Jamie, but I had my own life all worked out.

Liz and I dated for several years before we married. I did not have a lot to offer and it took quite some time and a loan from her parents before we could afford the trailer we first called home. It was a small unit, but I was thrilled with it. I had never had a shower before I moved in. Growing up, once a week, we heated water on the stove and every member of the family shared the same bathwater—the lucky ones got in first.

I loved Liz and was very happy, even more so at the birth of our beautiful daughter Ashley. Our standard of living, much improved from my childhood, was not what Liz hoped for. I promised her many times I would try to get a better job, but I never followed through. I was content and my lack of motivation to improve our situation frustrated Liz.

My idea of a good time was being home with my family, but Liz wanted more. She often went out with her girlfriends and Ashley and I, daddy and daughter, played happily together in our little nest. When Ashley was five, after almost thirteen years since we met at the roller rink, Liz filed for divorce. I was devastated.

The nights I did not have Ashley, I went to the bar. I could not stand being alone. I nursed the same beer for hours, then went home, threw myself on the carpet and cried. After a year of this, as I wallowed on the floor in my lonely efficiency, the Lord spoke to me. I did not hear an audible voice, but I knew deep in my spirit the words I heard, strong and clear. "You need to be baptized in Jesus' Name."

I called my brother, who in turn spoke with his pastor. I went to church and on Easter Sunday I obeyed the instruction God spoke to me in my brokenness. That small act of obedience was the turning point in my life—a point that began with a Word from God that lit the path He wanted me to take—a path toward freedom in Him. When I went down in the water a dejected, rejected man, I rose up with hope and a clean slate—a new beginning. A short time later I received the infilling of God's Spirit and the joy and peace His presence bring. The circumstances of my life did not change, but I did. God used the pain of divorce to reach to me with His gift of eternal life with Him and I can say without a doubt, that even though my life did not work out the way I hoped for or planned, life with God is the best life of all.

The Britches quilt pattern was said to be a symbol in a secondary quilt code that directed children on the Underground Railroad to receive fresh clothing from conductors along the way. To fleeing slaves of all ages, the pattern directed them to clothing that enabled them to blend into the community of freed people.

In Quilting Patches of Life, Volume I, I titled the story of a young father's diaper changing escapade Britches. When I discovered the pattern was said to be one used to communicate with runaway slaves, and Bill reminded me of the bellbottoms he and his brother shared, I could not resist titling this chapter Britches II.

I have a special interest in Bill's story—one you may have guessed if you looked at his last name, a name we now share. Bill and I worshipped together for three years before we married. When he first joined our church, I was married too…happily married to a wonderful man God chose to call home. Widowed at 32 with 2 small children, I worked through my own grief, but learned the same lesson Bill learned: that even when life doesn't work out as we expected, with God, life can still be good.

Individually, Bill and I traveled rough roads, in our childhoods and beyond. Together, we have journeyed yet more, but as Bill said, life with God is the best life of all, even when it comes with challenges. And on our journey, Bill and I were blessed with a daughter of our own—our little Hopey girl—the cheerful ribbon God used to tie our fractal family together. We all marveled at this precious gift, delighted in the smiling baby and the healing she brought into our lives. We watched when she learned to crawl across the carpet, her diapered bottom swaying over chubby legs, and we dubbed her "LBW—Little Britches Wagner." Hope is now eleven years old. She passed from a crawling "Little Britches Wagner" to a toddling "Hurricane Hope" and is now just a joy in our lives, a special girl, and a reminder to us of God's gift of restoration and hope.

CHAPTER 26
LOST CHILDREN

LaNaye Perkins - Olive Branch, Illinois

I sat alone in the recliner reading his note through tears. It was filled with sadness and despair—all the reasons my 23-year-old son had chosen to end his life. When my husband rushed him to the hospital, I was unable to go with him. Recuperating from the damage mold had inflicted, my lungs demanded a breathing treatment and there was no time to waste. So I stayed home and waited for news.

We live on a farm with family close by. Not wanting to draw attention to the house, I left most of the lights off to keep from alarming our neighbors, at least until I heard from my husband. I just could not bring myself to call anyone. Who could I call? What would I say? I could not even wrap my mind around what had happened, let alone try to explain it to anyone else. The only one I could talk to at that moment was Jesus.

Just one hour before, all was quiet in the house when I felt the Lord wake me from a sound sleep. I was strongly impressed with thoughts that my son was in trouble—that I should check on him. I climbed out of bed, a stranglehold of fear gripping my heart, and called out to him. "Can you come downstairs?" No answer.

I called him again, this time insisting he come down, unaware he had taken an overdose of pain killers and muscle relaxers. Thankfully, I persisted, otherwise my son would have fallen asleep and slipped from our lives forever. We would have passed through the night without us knowing anything happened until the following morning when we found the note he left by the coffee pot.

As I waited in the recliner in the darkened room, fear threatened to overwhelm me. Thoughts of a complete mental breakdown assaulted my mind, but in my spirit I knew I had to stay focused. I could not afford to give way to hysterics. I made myself continue in prayer, pleading with the Lord for my son's life. For nearly three hours, I battled fear and panic. Thank God for the Word that encouraged me during those difficult predawn hours.

One passage in particular spoke directly to me and this situation. "Be not afraid of sudden fear…for the Lord shall be thy confidence" (Proverbs 3:25-26). There were other verses, and I thanked the Lord for them all. As I read each one, they brought reassurance to my heart and strengthened my faith to keep believing for the best.

Nearly four hours had passed since my husband and son left for the hospital and I still had not received any news. For a long while I simply sat—quiet before the Lord—and then He spoke softly to my spirit. He let me know He would not have awakened me to watch my son die and with that, I knew that he would live.

The message came with a peace that wrapped around my soul like a physical embrace and defeated my fear. Fear fled in the presence of God's Spirit, His Word.

A short time later my husband called. "He's going to be okay," he said. And he was, physically, though the battle was not over.

For several months we all struggled to cope. Just how does a parent deal with the aftermath of child's suicide attempt—the near death of a life so precious to them? At first, our minds were so overwhelmed we could not think straight. All we could do was cry out to Jesus for help. We were tormented by scenarios of "what if," along with an intense condemnation that we had failed as parents.

Once the initial shock passed, we began searching the Bible for guidance. Reading the Scriptures helped us begin the healing process. During this time, the Lord comforted us with many verses and the power of His Word gave us faith to press on each day. In time, the Lord opened our eyes, affirming to my husband and me that we had done the best we could raising our children. We had to accept that our son, at 23 years of age, made his own choices that night.

After the suicide attempt, fear constantly undermined our faith, but we continued to cling to the Lord and the Word to see us through. One of the most helpful verses to me was, "I had fainted, unless I had believed to see the goodness of the LORD in the land of the living" (Psalm 27:13). It was only through God we overcame this consuming fear and found ourselves blessed with a peace we could not understand. We could not explain it, we just knew we had it.

The biggest of all obstacles sometimes comes in the form of a question. Why do tragedies happen? Why does life have to hurt—people have to hurt? Although the Lord often does not share the whys of life's challenges with His people, He does provide hope and purpose in every situation. "Blessed be God, even the Father of mercies, and the God of all comfort; Who comforteth us in all our tribulation, that we may be able to comfort them which are in any trouble, by the comfort wherewith we ourselves are comforted of God" (2 Corinthians 1:3-4). We can't say for certain why our family went through this trial, but we know that because of it, we can reach out to others. We can share with others what the Lord did for us. In turn, we can now help others in the same way we received help.

Today our son is doing great. He turned his life around and gives all the credit to God. Admittedly, there were times we felt this trial would kill us all, but God is faithful and we have learned to trust Him at a deeper level and walk in freedom from fear and condemnation.

ᡣᢧᠥᡣᠥ

I located a Lost Children pattern online as a block on a Civil War sampler quilt. The pattern, a four-pointed star assembled from multi-colored triangles, centers around a diamond square with a red cross in the middle. Looking over quilt patterns in the Civil War era, searching for the right name for LaNaye's story, the words "lost children" seemed to leap off the page. Surely everyone reading LaNaye's story knows someone dear to them who is "lost." For many, it may be their own child or spouse. Watching people we love make decisions that hurt themselves pains those who love them—sometimes more deeply than the "lost" one ever knows.

The war that brought an end to slavery, America's Civil War, set brother against brother, father against son, cousin against cousin, each risking life and limb for the principles they believed in...each believing God was on their side and using the Bible to back it up. That's fodder for a mountain of questions, but as LaNaye learned, we often don't get our whys answered. In the search to make sense of tragedy, our futile attempts to bring reason to the unreasonable forfeit our peace and confidence in God.

Slavery is a blight on American history. Nothing can erase the past and no amount of debate or rhetoric can bring honor to the deeds done against innocent men and women. Uncle Tom's Cabin, one of the most influential books in American history, although a work of fiction, gives insight to the many facets of slavery, from the slave owner to the enslaved. Though wicked men will be wicked, in every culture and society, many suffered under this system, slaves and slave-owners alike, both trapped in a system of bondage. And the lives and families broken to bring an end to the system devastated much of the population.

Thank God that in our nation, slavery is no longer the law of the land. And as we look back on the generations of the lost children of Africa and other far-away lands, as we remember those who lost their lives and loved ones in the Civil War conflict, may we realize that every person on earth is, or at one time was, a lost child in need of deliverance. Through Jesus' death on the cross, all mankind has an open pathway to God. That does not mean that all roads lead to God, but He will meet us on whatever path we are on and bring us the freedom that comes when He adopts us into the family of God. The choice is ours, and just like LaNaye's son who turned from a desolate self-inflicted death wish, we can turn to God for a victorious new life.

CHAPTER 27
BASKET

Debbie Roome – Christchurch, Canterbury, New Zealand

Mother of four children under the age of six, with number five soon on the way, my life and family changed forever when Ethel Zuma entered our home. We lived in South Africa for just over a year when we became aware the lovely woman who worked at our children's preschool as a cleaner was looking for accommodation. In exchange for help with ironing and cleaning, we offered her an outside room, and a few weeks after she moved in, she approached us with a question.

"I have a five year old son who lives with my mother in the rural areas. Can he come and live with me?"

Kevin and I discussed it that evening. Although we were slightly apprehensive, we agreed. We felt it was best for child and mother to be together and just hoped he would be well behaved.

Derrick, a quiet boy who spoke no English, arrived shortly thereafter. Our children accepted him straight away. Never having been exposed to modern city life, with their help, Derrick slowly adapted. It was an amusing process. At first he was terrified of us and insisted on sitting on the floor, never on our chairs. However, the TV and video machine were great attractions, as were the children's toys. His confidence grew and within a year, he spoke perfect English and attended Christian school with our children.

Ethel was comfortable with the part our family played in Derrick's life, so we continued to include him in family activities. We took him on his first trip to the beach and he learned to swim in our pool. On special occasions he went out with us to restaurants and he began attending our church.

When Derrick was about nine, we decided to visit his family home in Impendle, a rural area about ninety minutes from the city where we lived. The tar road soon deteriorated into a muddy track, and we bounced through pot holes and drove cautiously through swollen streams. Finally, after dropping into a valley, we wound among hundreds of round mud dwellings until Ethel pointed out their home, a cluster of four huts and a chicken shed on a scraggly square of grass.

The Zumas were excited to have visitors and showed us around their patch of land. One of the huts was the kitchen and communal area where they ate and socialized. Cooking was done on an ancient wood stove Ethel's mother was very proud of. The other huts were sleeping quarters for the grandparents and extended family members. It was immediately apparent they owned very little—no electricity, no running water, little food and not much clothing.

It was on that visit we decided to gather some goodies together and make a return trip. Over the next few months we collected used clothing and stockpiled boxes of food. Ethel's mother, recently hospitalized for malnutrition, was in dire need of the basics such as corn meal, peanut butter and beans. We also gathered treats like biscuits, bottles of fizzy drinks, oats, porridge and syrup.

Taking our gifts to the family was a life-changing experience. In many ways I think my family benefited more than Ethel's. The expressions on their faces were priceless and we have many rich memories of those days. I will never forget how Derrick trapped rats, roasted them over a fire and shared them with our children. I remember the neighboring families decimated by violence and AIDS, and grandmothers struggling to raise a dozen grandchildren. I recall with pleasure sharing the Zuma's joy over a newly installed tap that worked one hour per day. They insisted on killing one of their few chickens and cooking it for us. My husband and I sat on their two rickety chairs while they sat on a grass mat. Under the midday African sun, we shared bowls of tough, stringy chicken and cups of warm cola. Although Derrick and Ethel had to translate, we felt accepted and content in their company.

The years passed and Derrick became more and more a part of our family—a brother to our children and a son to us. If he misbehaved, we discussed the situation with Ethel, and if necessary a good hiding followed. It was a joy when he gave his life to Jesus, and as he moved into his teens, his gifts began to develop. I taught him to play bass guitar and got him going on the piano. By the time he was 18, he was leading praise and worship at school and church. In 2005, his last year at school, he was elected as a prefect, alongside our daughter who was head girl.

That was our last year in South Africa. We heard God's voice calling us to New Zealand and knew we had to say very painful goodbyes to Ethel, Derrick and our family. Kevin left three months before the rest of us. Following are some excerpts from the card Derrick gave him that day.

Dear Uncle Kevin,

It's been 14 years since I moved in to live alongside your family! I have known you for most of my life and you have become like a father to me.

My quiet times in the morning were inspired by you. How you wake up early to pray almost every day with such a sincere heart.

Thank you also for your hospitality and for the many friends of mine that you have allowed into your house. And most of all, thank you for showing such goodness and love towards my family.

May the Lord always turn His face towards you and give you peace. Thank you for everything.

Love from Derrick and Ethel

In January 2006, our five children and I left South Africa. It broke our hearts to leave Derrick behind.

My parents now employ Ethel, and Derrick works as a music teacher in a Christian school. We keep in touch and recently heard he bought himself a car. He earns extra money singing and playing guitar. Other friends tell us he has blossomed and is doing well.

Our years in South Africa were not particularly happy ones and on arriving in New Zealand I asked God why we could not have come straight here from Zimbabwe. Why we had to spend 15 years in difficult circumstances. His answer was immediate and clear. Those years were to give Derrick a chance at a better life. To lead him to God and help him become a man of influence. I don't know what lies ahead for Derrick, but I know God has a definite plan for his life. A plan my family was, and are, privileged to be part of.

❦

Having enough to eat was one of the most difficult challenges runaway slaves faced. After consuming what they were able to gather and carry along with them, they depended on the generosity of others—primarily friends in safe houses. In addition to shelter and transportation, abolitionists regularly provided baskets of food and other items, like flints and compasses, to help fugitives along their way.

A Basket quilt hanging outside a house is said to have indicated a location where a basket of provisions could be obtained or a place fugitive slaves could hide until food was brought to them. Women often carried life-saving supplies in the bottom of laundry and sewing baskets that disguised their missions.

Many variations of the Basket pattern exist today, but the most common pieced block is made of half square triangle units with rectangles and single triangles mixed in to complete the block. Baskets have been used as decorative symbols throughout our nation's history, memorializing their importance in the day-to-day lives of people from all walks of life. In our world, baskets have largely been replaced with paper bags and plastic laundry tubs—even eco-friendly reusable fabric bags, but baskets still serve as symbols of our love for hearth and home, and are often used as containers for gifts of all kinds.

When the Roomes employed Ethel and she asked permission for her son to join her, no one knew the impact her request would have on the lives of all those involved. As I read the story of Debbie's family gathering their goodies in boxes for others who lacked basic necessities, I thought of the Basket quilt pattern and how it represented provision for those in need.

The Roomes may not have recognized it at the time, but beyond the kind giving of food and clothing boxed and distributed to Ethel's family, they filled another empty container God sent their way—a five-year old boy named Derrick. Over the years, they placed their gifts inside the "basket" of Derrick's life—nurturing him and filling him with godly examples of Christianity in action, familial love and acceptance. Derrick's vessel was filled by God's provision through the Roome family, and who knows whose baskets Derrick will fill from the bounty he received?

"That this nation, under God, shall have a
new birth of freedom – and that government of
the people, by the people, for the people,
shall not perish from the earth."
– Abraham Lincoln

CHAPTER 28
MAPLE LEAF

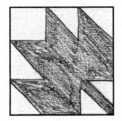

Karen Skolney - Kelvington, Saskatchewan, Canada

I will just say it, I was into witchcraft—and I didn't even realize it. I read the Bible and prayed to Jesus, all the while I channeled, communicated with spirits and engaged in other occult practices. Somehow I confused witchcraft with spirituality and as a result lived in guilt, fear and confusion. Oddly, I believed what I was doing was okay and in the small town of Wishart, Saskatchewan, no one told me anything different.

My family knew very little of what I was doing. Married with children, I had all four of my little ones baptized as infants in both the Roman Catholic and Lutheran churches, just to cover all the bases.

One night, before my family moved from Wishart, I had a horrific dream. In it, my husband and I drove a beat up truck down an old country road in the middle of nowhere. Of all things, we were hauling a crate of pigs. We drove into a forest, the murky light darkening as we traveled. Just as visibility dimmed to impassible, we came upon a cabin where we stopped for the night. We slept, but I was jarred awake by terrified squeals outside the cabin. I jumped out of bed, looked out the window and saw huge bearded lions killing the pigs. They weren't eating them. They just killed one and moved on to the next, and when they realized I saw them, they strode menacingly toward the cabin. The closer they came, the thinner and more worn out the cabin grew until little separated me from the beasts closing in. Their eyes glowed red with evil. The biggest one roared and leapt toward me.

I woke from the nightmare screaming and scrambled out of bed panting and shaking. For several weeks, a residual terror kept me from restful sleep. It seemed the lion from my dream became a part of me and I saw it every time I closed my eyes.

Our family moved to Kelvington, where we began attending a Spirit-filled church. The pastor had his work cut out for him. We had so much to learn. But as we studied the Word, I knew I wanted to be baptized. We set the date, and I could hardly wait for the big day—one of two special events upcoming: first the wedding of my school mate, Karen, and then my baptism.

The week before Karen's wedding in Outlook, my van's tired old power steering pump popped a hose and all the fluid drained off. My husband fixed it as best as he could, and I ordered a new one, assured it would be in on time for the trip. The morning we were scheduled to leave, I took the van in to get the part installed. The attendant checked the courier packages, and surprise…no pump! His receipt indicated the part was shipped, but it was not with the rest of the parcels.

My husband had left the day before for work and the van was my only means of transportation. I felt terrible about missing Karen's wedding and phoned her to break the news. We both had a little cry, but she said she understood.

After we hung up, I thought, "What's the worst that could happen?" So on impulse and a prayer, I packed up the kids, and we headed to Outlook early Friday morning. "Jesus," I prayed along the way, "Please keep my power steering pump working."

The wedding was beautiful, the first I had attended in an Apostolic church and the bride and groom simply glowed. After the ceremony, we went to the lower level for the reception. Everyone was talking and laughing and I wondered at how happy everyone was at this alcohol-free celebration.

Seated across the table from Karen's pastor and his wife, Don and Lois McQuinn, I talked with them about God. Sister Lois asked if I would like to pray, and to my surprise, we held hands and prayed right there. For the first time in my life, I felt God's presence, but as we prayed, I realized there was a huge blockage between me and something wonderful.

The McQuinn's son Mitchell, recently home from Bible College, suggested we go upstairs to pray further. I agreed, but was not prepared for what happened next. I closed my eyes, and as Sister Lois began praying, I saw a fierce lion leap out at me. I fell to my knees frightened and sobbing.

Sister Lois knew what to do. She spoke to the lion and commanded it to leave in Jesus' Name. She then told me to do the same. I did. And you know what? It left.

I closed my eyes again, and this time I saw another lion—a brilliant, magnificent one much bigger than the first. I can't say for certain, but I've often thought of that second lion as the Lion of the Tribe of Judah—a manifestation of Jesus. Sister Lois said later the only thing a lion is afraid of is a bigger lion.

I thanked Sister Lois for her prayers and shared with her my plans to be baptized on Sunday. Together, we opened the Bible and read Scriptures about baptism. We read lots of passages and when we got to Acts 2:38, the words seemed to jump off the page and into my heart. I heard a voice inside say, "This is good!" I wanted it, and I wanted it right then. "We have a tank and lots of water to fill it," Sister Lois said.

With a mix of hope and hesitation, I looked at Karen and her new husband. "This is your day, Karen," I said. "How can I do this and take away from your wedding day?" She looked at me and said, "No. This is the day that the Lord hath made."

After preparations, I stepped into the tank, more excited than I had ever been, and Pastor Don baptized me in the Name of Jesus! I came up out of the water, raised my hands in worship and began speaking in a different language. Everyone was rejoicing around me and I was overcome with emotion. I knew I was a new person and I've never been the same since.

I was free—free from the chains of false religion—witchcraft is a religion, after all. I was free from the torment that had plagued my life. And although I know there will always be more to learn about God, I am now free to have a personal relationship with Him. Whom the Son sets free is free indeed (John 8:36).

The Maple Leaf quilt pattern, though not part of the "Quilt Code," represents Canada, the fleeing slave's ultimate destination. Generally made in only two colors, blocks are comprised of one focus fabric and one background fabric. Lighter in hue, the background's variation from the darker inner pieces brings a clear delineation of the pattern, the form of the leaf easily discerned. Without the marked contrast, the pattern would be difficult to make out.

Karen's story relates to the Maple Leaf pattern in several ways. The block represents the physical move of fleeing slaves to a new location in the northern country. And like Karen, who made her own Canadian move, refugees also clung to the hope of a new life of freedom—a life in high contrast to the one lived as the property of another man.

Beyond the physical comparisons, this story connects pattern and person in a much deeper way. Spirituality is real, in all its forms. Many people willing to embrace the reality of angels reject the possibility of their fallen peers. If the Bible is true, and I believe it is and has been proven to be so, heavenly angels exist—demonic spirits, as well. As Karen's spiritual understanding opened, as Truth dawned, the realization of the marked contrast between a holy God and occult darkness came first with terror, but ultimately with freedom and peace. When Karen looked into the Word, she found the "lines" the Lord had drawn—lines that marked a clear pattern for her to follow, even when she stepped into the waters of baptism.

I remember with joy the day of my baptism and the freedom from the weight that fell away, the new sense of lightness in the core of my being. Within the sanctuary walls, the sun seemed to shine down on me, radiating the love of God in a way I had never known possible.

The Maple Leaf pattern, often done in the dark colors of the Fall season, indicates a passage of time. Regardless the season of life, we all have equal access to this wonderful cleansing from God. One of my favorite hymns, *Great is Thy Faithfulness,* shares the message: "Summer, and winter, springtime and harvest"…God is faithful. "Pardon for sin and a peace that endureth"…with God all people have the hope of new life, a new beginning with Him, and new mercies every morning (Lamentations 3:22-23).

Great is thy faithfulness
O God my Father
There is no shadow of turning with Thee;
Thou changest not, Thy compassions, they fail not;
As Thou hast been, Thou forever will be.

Great is Thy faithfulness!
Great is Thy faithfulness!
Morning by morning new mercies I see.
All I have needed Thy hand hath provided;
Great is Thy faithfulness, Lord, unto me!

Summer and winter and springtime and harvest,
Sun, moon and stars in their courses above
Join with all nature in manifold witness
To Thy great faithfulness, mercy and love.

Pardon for sin and a peace that endureth
Thine own dear presence to cheer and to guide;
Strength for today and bright hope for tomorrow,
Blessings all mine, with ten thousand beside!

Words: Thomas O. Chisholm
Music: "Faithfulness (Runyan)," William M. Runyan

"So many people live in a self-imposed slavery because they've been betrayed by selfish lovers. God wants to heal our wounds and bring us to a place of living free in a loving relationship with Him."
— Carey Kinsolving

CHAPTER 29
BUTTERFLY

Bonnie Winters – Philipsburg, Pennsylvania

"Thanks, I'll watch this tonight." I pasted on a smile for my home-health supervisor and slipped the training video in my bag, promising to return it the next day. Unable to attend the in-service training, I was required to watch the session to keep my certification to work with developmentally disabled clients.

Arriving home, I turned the videotape over in my hands and blew out my frustration. "I have so much to do, when am I supposed to have time to watch this before tomorrow?" I groaned as I mentally ticked items off my list. "I'll have to fight with the kids for the TV, cook supper, do the dishes and get ready to teach tonight at church. When I come home, I have to put everyone to bed and finish getting things ready for tomorrow." I was certain I would not have any energy left to absorb the information on the video.

All my mental whining seemed unnecessary when the kids went outside to play and left me a free hour to watch the video before supper. "I might as well get this over with," I thought. "At least this one sounds interesting–therapy for children with cerebral palsy."

I was soon caught up in the story. A therapist worked with a child who had severe CP. Her arms and legs drawn tightly to her body reminded me of my children's egg-shaped toy figures that wobbled and rocked on the floor. An aide sat behind her and steadied the child as she tried to stay upright. At times she gently pressed on her legs to help her stay balanced and loosen muscles.

A therapist sat in front of the child, holding out various toys and snacks to tempt her to reach for them. All the while, he softly crooned encouragement at each attempt to stretch her rigid muscles. When the girl became frustrated, he continued to encourage with soft words, sometimes physically grasping her limbs and gently coaxing them to stretch as she reached toward her goal. Several hours each day were spent in painful therapy to keep the child from losing mobility.

After a few minutes, the scene switched to a little boy with a different type of CP. He had no muscle tone at all and was unable to move by himself. He lay like a limp rag doll while the therapist manipulated his muscles for several hours each day attempting to re-pattern his brain and muscles to work together.

I was surprised at how much the video moved me. I watched it a second time and throughout the evening powerful images of the children returned, stirring my heart again.

The next morning, during my half hour commute, I spent the first few miles pondering the gripping scenes from the video. I wondered how I could use the things I learned. I had primarily watched the video for in-service credit and was doubtful I would have the opportunity to try that type of work.

As I reached the outskirts of the city, my thoughts took their own lead and turned down a path to another kind of therapy—the heavy-duty emotional workout I encountered each week. My participation in this group was one of the hardest things I had ever done. In each intense session, seven participants and I gathered with a psychotherapist and his wife, a psychiatric nurse, to work through issues related to childhood sexual abuse.

It took me several weeks to build enough trust to discuss the issues I faced—damaged sexuality, unhealthy ways of relating to the world around me, and low self-esteem. From childhood, I had been conditioned to be silent about those issues—a silence that left me spiritually and emotionally bound.

Suddenly, the Lord spoke to my heart so clearly it was as though He were sitting right beside me. "You are like those children with cerebral palsy. Your ability to trust Me has been damaged by the abuse you suffered as a child."

In one of those light bulb moments, I understood. Though I had been a Christian from a young age, my trust muscles had atrophied because of the damage from the abuse. Despite all the scriptural affirmations that God was a loving Father who delights in giving good gifts to His children, I could not accept the idea that my wants and needs mattered. I secretly feared I annoyed Him, that He might just get fed up with me and cast me aside.

The scenes from the video flashed in my memory again, but this time I was the child with CP, my arms and legs tight against my body. Fear kept me from reaching out to trust a loving Savior. I sensed the gentle warmth of the Holy Spirit surrounding me, steadying me so I would not tumble over. Jesus sat before me, encouraging and enticing me to reach for Him, to trust Him, speaking soft, gentle words. His tone was patient, unhurried and above all, not bothered by my paralyzing fear of trust. Each time I made the least effort to stretch toward Him, His words came, softly urging me to reach a little farther, a little higher.

Like the developmentally disabled children, I knew I would require many hours of painful therapy to loosen those atrophied trust muscles. God had already laid the groundwork for trust between the members of my therapy group. It had become a safe haven where I felt valuable and loved unconditionally. Now it was up to me to commit to the painful healing process of opening my heart. The Great Therapist wanted to cleanse and heal the hurts as my friends gathered around to help me stretch and grow spiritually.

The Lord reminded me of the patience of the therapist in the video. He did not get frustrated with the child, but kept encouraging gently with soft words and calm movements. He was aware of her pain and her needs, never causing the child to feel like a burden or a bother. Then He spoke to me again. "Child, you are worth the time and energy I am investing in you."

In that precious, life-changing moment, I finally understood. God would work patiently with me, helping me grow into a trusting, mature believer no matter how long it took—because He loved me.

The healing process took over four years. Through that time, I sensed His presence before me, gently guiding, encouraging and loving me patiently as I learned to stretch out my damaged trust muscles to my Heavenly Father, emotionally and spiritually free at last.

Many variations exist of Butterfly quilt patterns. Pieced blocks and appliquéd patterns in vibrant colors adorn quilts created in the last two centuries. Boxy wings, curved wings, variegated wings, flowery wings, opened wings—every Butterfly quilt reminds us of the beauty of nature, and one particular spiritual message God planted within the life cycle of the butterfly.

The writings of Harriet Beecher Stowe helped galvanize the abolitionist cause. *Uncle Tom's Cabin* sold over 10,000 copies its first week of publication and is still available in reprints today. According to legend, Abraham Lincoln attributed the outbreak of the Civil War to the author. "So you're the little woman who wrote the book that started this Great War!" the President is credited with saying at their meeting in 1862.

Beecher Stowe, in a sub-story in this classic work, wrote of a wretched slave catcher, who ironically shared the same name as the book's hero. Unlike the enslaved, peaceable, God-fearing Uncle Tom, this man hunted humanity for hire. Injured in a chase and left in the care of a Quaker woman, Tom cursed and complained saying he was too hot under the goodwoman's quilts. The woman lifted the quilt and patiently tucked a lighter covering around him, all the while ministering to his spirit with her sweet ways. The book's narrator remarked that Tom looked like a chrysalis wrapped in so completely under the sheeting.

During his confinement, fighting fever and pain, the injured man fought both physically and spiritually. Lying in his chrysalis, unable to move or care for himself, Tom underwent a metamorphosis that changed his life. He chose to turn away from his past and provided information that led to the successful escape of the slaves he had been chasing. He began a new life in the northern country among the Quakers.

Encased in an invisible yet binding covering, Bonnie experienced a metamorphosis of her own. Like a caterpillar, she had grown to a point of change. Butterfly larva search out a safe place, anchor themselves to growing surfaces and transform into chrysalis. Unseen in the caterpillar stage, miniature wings on the outside of the chrysalis absorb a great deal of nutrients and transform into large, flight-capable appendages. When God opened Bonnie's understanding, she embarked on her own journey of transformation. Ready to change, she found the safe place of her therapy group, anchored herself to the Word God had given her, and over time, as she absorbed the spiritual nutrients of Word and Spirit, found the freedom that eluded her so many years. May every one reading hear God's voice and respond as beautifully as Bonnie, who with God's help, now flies free from the pain of the past on the wings of love's liberty.

Freedom begins with Jesus. Jesus is the way, the truth, and the life. If we know Jesus, we will know truth that sets us free. "They shall know the Truth and the Truth shall set them free" (John 8:32).

CHAPTER 30
BIRD IN THE AIR

Anne Linington – Totland Bay, Isle of Wight, United Kingdom

I dangled at the end of a rope, halfway up a steep rock-face. I had been afraid this would happen, careful with every move of a hand or foot to avoid losing my grip and the terror of falling down the side of a cliff. As I hung suspended between the top of the great rock and the earth below, my instructor, out of sight, held the rope fastened to the cliff above. Now, after all the assurances received and precautions taken, I learned for myself I could trust the security of the rope.

Several months earlier, I applied for one of four annual scholarships to an Outward Bound Activity Centre. When I learned I was chosen to receive funds from the local benefactor, I knew little of the challenges ahead of me but looked forward to four weeks of canoeing, rock-climbing, orienteering and assault courses.

Our foursome, all 17 years of age, traveled by train to the West Wales coast. We negotiated several changes before we arrived at Rhowniar Outward Bound Centre where we disembarked and dispersed into different dormitories. We were not among the first to check in and we found many of the bunks already taken. The number of police cadets from large cities, like Liverpool, surprised me. I was a quiet school girl from Devon, a new Christian pleased to just find a quiet place to read my Bible. I felt as if I had been thrown in the deep end of a pool.

I began extensive preparations for the trip several weeks before the scheduled departure date. Time and resources were spent gathering the things I needed for the trip and I began applying surgical spirit, per instructions, to toughen up my feet. To this day, surgical spirit instantly reminds me of camping stoves and sore feet.

For my kit, I needed several pair of trousers and purchased a brand new pair of climbing boots. Colorful cotton and woolen socks were knit for me in royal blue, bright green and red. Perhaps, I thought, my socks would be spotted if I got lost. Regardless the reason, I remember the horror I felt at their first washing when the colors ran profusely.

One of the greatest challenges we faced was the assault course. We jumped high in the trees from one branch to another. Although the leaps were only a few inches apart, the many feet off the ground made each attempt frightening yet exhilarating. Canoeing lessons began with a purposeful capsizing to learn to breathe the air in the space beneath the upturned boat. I faced my fear of being under water and the pain brought on by an earlier eardrum perforation.

I was keen on geography, so I particularly enjoyed the orienteering, using a map and compass to plot a route and reach a planned destination. This was a group activity with each of us taking turns to lead and an assessment given of our leadership skills afterward.

Other activities involved a three-day hike. After careful planning, we packed and carried all our camping equipment as we covered some forty miles of challenging terrain. A climb to a rocky summit with the most spectacular view, the highlight of the hike, made all the effort worthwhile.

For some reason, probably enhanced by the good-looking instructor, I most relished the challenges of rock climbing and abseiling. At times we faced rocky outcrops and at others, coastal cliffs. The most frightening descent took us by surprise when we discovered a cave at the base. The unforeseen difficulties increased the challenge, but we learned to respond to the unexpected.

I learned the greatest lesson on the day I fell. A group of us ascended the cliff using ropes and carabiners. As we had been taught, we moved one limb at a time—consistently keeping three points of contact with the rock. Somehow I slipped; whether I overstretched or simply missed my footing, I do not know, but I lost my grip and began falling, hurtling to the ground. After a sharp jar, the rope strained under my ribs and I found myself suspended in mid air. In that terrifying moment, I realized the rope held. I was safe. Dangling at the end of the rope, I received a new level of confidence. The fall, as scary as I imagined, actually liberated me from my fear.

My instructors reassured me and I took a few moments to find new holds for my hands and feet, then began my ascent again. Everything was different this time. Despite being shaken by the fall, the mental changes were remarkable. My worst fear had been faced and the rope had held fast. I climbed with renewed confidence and much greater enjoyment knowing that if the worst happened, I might be bruised, but I would live.

I really appreciated the lesson I learned that day and have used it as an illustration to share with others about God. Though we cannot see Him, He keeps us safe, even when we fall.

⸙

Quaker abolitionists Lindley and Debra Coates ran a safe house in Lancaster County, Pennsylvania. To aid fugitives traveling on the Underground Railroad, Debra designed the first Birds in the Air directional quilt. Symbolic of flight or migration, the quilt was created with a dominant color that indicated direction. Coates displayed the quilt so that its blocks pointed the way fugitives should travel on their journeys to freedom.

Over the years quilters modified the Birds In The Air pattern, also called Bird in the Air, but although the designs vary, they all are made exclusively with triangles.

At the young age of 17, Anne learned a lesson that will see her through the years ahead. The unseen hands of her instructor kept Anne safe, even when she took a misstep or slipped along the way. Our God is just like that. He is our lifeline. He is our rock. He is everything we need.

We all face times we feel out of control—when we sense the Lord asks us to trust Him beyond what seems safe or reasonable.

Sometimes we experience momentary jolts or sudden fears, and sometimes we face extreme or lengthy challenges.

Abseiling, or rappelling, is the controlled descent down a rope when a slope is too steep or dangerous to descend unprotected. When I looked at all the equipment necessary—helmets, boots, harnesses and so on, it reminded me of the armor of God (Ephesians 6). To maneuver safely around the challenges in our lives, we need to have the right equipment, both to take ground, and protect us along the way. No matter what we face, even if we lose our grip and fall, the rope of our faith is able to keep us secure in God.

CHAPTER 31
BLAZING STAR OF KENTUCKY

Cheryl Yates — Paducah, Kentucky

W hen I was a kid my friends and sisters and I used to play on the railroad tracks near our house. We walked for miles, and as long as I had a companion, the time passed quickly. Alone, one mile would have seemed unending.

John lived just around the corner. He was probably my best friend in those days. We played games on his screened-in porch with his sister and mine while his gray-haired, apron-clad mother served us lemonade.

John's family lived in an old farmhouse with a large bell mounted on a pole outside the back door. Perhaps in earlier years the bell called children for lemonade or farmers in for supper—but not anymore. Now it was just a novelty in a developing subdivision.

Though many houses were being built all around us, John's family owned a fair-sized piece of land with a creek and several outbuildings in which we freely created mischief—like the time John's sister and mine set up a haunted house. It was broad daylight, sunlight beaming in the windows, but the container of spaghetti they told me were brains still petrified me. I bolted out the door of the cinder-block building and would not go back in, sick to my stomach and wondering where they found those brains.

Next to our house, across the gravel drive, our neighbor Josephine lived in an old white house. Josephine, an older lady, didn't like being pestered by kids, so my sisters and I usually kept our distance. Just in case we forgot, she had a dog named Dolly who quickly reminded us. Dolly looked pretty from a distance, with fluffy white hair and a curly tail, but I will never forget the sight of those gums pulled back quivering across her fangs when I got too close to the house.

Josephine had a large hill in her front yard that my sisters and I played on. It was close enough to our driveway, I suppose, that we felt we had a right to it. She also had several rows of daffodils we felt we had a right to as well, after all, they were only inches from our driveway. My older sister learned to ride her bike coming down the grassy hill of Josephine's yard where it ran into our driveway. At the end of the field behind her house, a giant oak tree stood—a favorite site for playing ring-around-the-rosy and other games. With such events taking place right in her very own yard, I wondered why Josephine didn't like kids.

One day a tall, slender man wearing a Sunday hat sat alone on Josephine's porch and I snuck over to meet him (something I would never have done if Dolly had been out). "Who are you?" I asked the man. "I'm Andy," he said. "Josephine's brother. I'll be living here with her now." Andy was such a nice man. I stole over to see him every chance I could.

Josephine loved gourds and had quite a collection hanging about her yard. I'm not really sure why, but those gourds used to frighten me; the dirty, earthy color and unpredictable shapes...and those mysterious holes drilled in them. In a way I was intrigued, but mostly scared. One day Josephine took me to her root cellar and showed me how she dried the gourds and turned them into bird houses, painting them baby blue when they were ready. Josephine sure seemed nice that day, and I suppose every day from then on.

The last time I was in Josephine's house I stood on a big, red Persian rug in a room full of antiques. "Here," Josephine said as she walked into the room where I had been waiting and handed me a harmonica. "Andy wanted you to have this. He knew you liked music." I didn't understand where Andy was but gladly accepted the gift and went outside to play with it.

Often, only time puts things in perspective. Andy must have seen something budding in this music teacher that I never saw back then. And Josephine? Well, she may have seemed like a mean, little old lady at one time, but when I showed interest in her bird houses, all that changed.

Children are so self-absorbed. If I could only go back and show her how much I care about other things now too. About her brother dying, and about destroying all the hard work she put into those flower beds. But Josephine is gone, as is the house she used to live in, and the giant hill that used to lay beyond our drive. The last time I looked it was just a tiny slope.

About a year ago curiosity led me down the old street, past Josephine's place and around the corner to see John's old farmhouse. It was completely surrounded by houses that seemed to have popped up overnight like mushrooms. The bell was still there, but it sure looked a lot smaller. And though a lot was different, a lot was just exactly the same. I suppose the same could be said of me.

It's good to remember those days when I was younger. Before I knew about labor, and hardship and trouble, I freely enjoyed the sunshine in fields of bluegrass under the clear Kentucky sky—going wherever the railroad tracks led me—to my friend's or the Minit-Mart. Remembering those days brings a much-needed balance to my thoughts, a balance I was missing since my parents' divorce.

Despite the ways I've often remembered my childhood, my life hasn't been all bad. I recall feeling like a wishbone being pulled from both sides, destined to be broken by the very hands I desperately wanted to cling to. It seemed whichever parent got the bigger half got to keep me, but I know now we were all broken. There was no winner. Still, treasured moments from my early youth stand as evidence against the somber memories, and I'm happy to have that objection.

I miss my father. He's been gone for many years now, but God has reminded me of good days and experiences I would not have had if life had played out differently. I treasure memories of sleepovers at my grandparents' house, playing with Grandma's empty wooden spools and listening to Grandpa play Turkey In The Straw on the harmonica. I enjoyed playing with all my cousins the times we stayed at my aunts and uncles' homes even as my parents struggled through a difficult divorce, and all the many other activities and relationships that filled otherwise dark days. It wasn't a fair trade, but I did get something out of the deal. And I still carry those memories with me everywhere I go, clinging to them just as tightly as I did to my parent's hands, clinging most of all to the Word that gives me hope and purpose.

"And we know that all things work together for good to them that love God, to them who are the called according to His purpose" (Romans 8:28).

❦

The Blazing Star of Kentucky is a variation of the easily recognizable pre-civil war Lone Star quilt pattern. Fabric diamonds form star points that radiate from the center in an eight-point design that commonly variegates from dark to light in a sunburst effect. The large star spans the quilt top, often with smaller stars pieced in the blank fields surrounding it.

A second Blazing Star design is made of four-pointed star blocks pieced from diamonds formed by two contrasting fabric triangles creating a pinwheel effect. In yet a third pattern of the same name, small Lone Stars blocks repeat across the quilt top.

Named after a tavern on the roadway linking New York and Philadephia, modern day Rossville, Staten Island, was previously known as Blazing Star. Around 1850, Dr. Samuel McKenzie Elliot, a well known abolitionist, built a gabled stone home in the area that was said to feature a tunnel from its cellar to the waterfront—a station on the Underground Railroad.

Once slavery was abolished, freedmen as far away as Maryland and Virginia joined with those from around the state to settle the area in the southwest corner and work the oyster trade. This area, Sandy Ground, is the oldest continuously inhabited free black community in the nation.

Decaying pieces of wood from an old pier mark the remains of the Blazing Star Ferry, and an eerie boat graveyard hosts tugs, barges and skiffs of decades past lingering in varying stages of decrepitude—a fleet of ships carrying hundreds of tales in one moment of time.

My sister Cheryl's story certainly brought back memories. I confess, she has a much better retention for long past details than I, but as she shared, I relived many of the events through her recollections. I had forgotten Josephine's flower garden, but could never forget the beautiful, frightful Dolly. The haunted house escapade escapes my memory, but I clearly recall the curve in the road to John's house and that Cheryl spent much time there before our parents' divorce when she was 10 and I was 11. As I read, melancholy mingled with sweet reminiscence of innocent childhood shenanigans.

It's often easy to look upon an incident and recall only pain or loss, but I thank God that my sisters and I have tucked away special memories—our own "blazing stars" that ignite happy thoughts and smatter bits of light across the dark sky of our season of sorrow. Taking a last look at the different Blazing Star quilt patterns, I pondered the formation of each design…how each variation was made of diamonds… and how natural diamonds form under the pressure of dark earth. Eventually mined, cleaned and brought forth, diamonds reflect the blazing light of the great star, our sun, and bring beauty to our world. May we do the same.

"We must have the faith that things will work out somehow, that God will make a way for us when there seems no way."
– Martin Luther King

CHAPTER 32

GOING AROUND THE MOUNTAIN

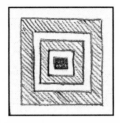

Bob and Linda Welch – Warren, Michigan

In 1992, only one year after coming to the Lord, my husband received a terrible diagnosis. Cancer had invaded his throat and lymph nodes, and the prognosis was grim. Our doctor predicted Bob had only four months to live.

Still in shock, we met with a second doctor. He advised us to have another test conducted to locate the root of the cancer. This information would assist the surgeon attempting to remove the affected cells. The test revealed the location, and we scheduled a date for surgery. Bob came through the operation and immediately began radiation and chemotherapy treatments.

From the beginning, we prayed as a family. As hard as things were, we knew somehow that through it all, God was with us. Treatments ravaged Bob's body in attempt to heal it of disease. I remember one point in particular he was so sick he felt he could hardly go on. In this time of great weakness, God showed our family how very strong He really is.

Though weak in body, Bob maintained a strong faith in God and from the valley of sickness and fatigue, he rallied his spirit with remarkable fortitude. On the way to his radiation treatments, Bob gave praise to God. This totally confused the staff at the hospital. People asked him why he was praising God, and he had the wonderful opportunity to tell them about Jesus. He shared with many that our God is great, even in not-so-great circumstances and that the Lord was with him always, even during radiation treatments.

Bob is not a preacher, but he knew where his strength was coming from and was willing to share that with others. We still experienced some rough times—dealing with cancer and cancer treatments was not easy, and watching a loved one suffer hurts deeply. I thank God that Bob made it through treatments to a full recovery, and now, 17 years later and cancer free, we are grateful for each day.

But the story does not end there. In 2005, I too received a diagnosis of cancer. It was Stage 3 colon cancer and I was immediately scheduled for surgery. Doctors removed a foot and a half of my colon and I went through a regimen of chemotherapy treatments. An adverse reaction to my first chemo treatment came close to taking my life, but the doctors adjusted the medications and I tolerated treatments a bit better.

Through it all, I suffered with extreme sickness, nausea and fatigue. Like Bob, during my treatments I leaned on our big God to see me through. At times life seemed surreal, almost as though God closed me off from the real world and hid me with Him much of the time. He tucked me safely under His wing and as we did throughout Bob's illness, we again regularly prayed Psalm 91.

Praying this Scripture reminded me that regardless of my circumstances, I still had access to a place of safety, a "secret place of the most High." This place of refuge promised freedom from night terrors and daytime trials. I clung to the promise that no plague would come near my home, that God would set angels to watch over me to keep my in all my ways, even in a cancer treatment center. Above all, verse 15 assured me that God would be with me in trouble and He would deliver me somehow.

Four years have passed since doctors declared me cancer free. Throughout the trials of our sicknesses, God repeatedly used our church family to bless Bob and me. They supported us continually in prayer. Our children and family also came through in such precious ways—ways Bob and I know God used to meet needs that saw us through this difficult time. I just do not know how we would have made it through without them.

My husband and I learned, and want to share with others, that no matter what happens in this life, Jesus holds our hands through it all and leads us through the valley of the shadow of the death. We did not know how our stories would turn out (only God knew that), but take it from two cancer survivors—God brings blessings in the middle of our rocky roads. God is great and I encourage everyone to worship Him with every ounce of energy you have. Be blessed and know God is with you always!

❦

In addition to the quilts in the "Quilt Code," many other patterns link to the pre-civil war era and the practice of slavery, as well. The Going Around the Mountain pattern reminded me of the negro spiritual *Climbin' Up D' Mountain* and could easily share the same graphic design. Going Around the Mountain, a whole-top design, starts around a square or rectangle. Like the popular Log Cabin pattern, single-colored rows of patches march around the center, the rows varying in shades of lights and darks until they reach the outer edge.

Songs, often used to transmit hidden messages along the Underground Railroad, offered a safe communication system wherever slaves lived or worked. In full sight and hearing of overseers, lyrics delivered greetings and instructions. The first lines of *Climbin' Up D' Mountain* seem to issue its own farewell message.

Climbin' up d' mountain, children
Didn't come here to stay
And if I nevermore see you again
Gonna meet you at de judgment day

Hebrew in de fiery furnace
And dey begin to pray
And de good Lawd smote dat fire out
Oh, wasn't dat a mighty day!
Good Lord, wasn't dat a mighty day!

Daniel went in de lions den
And he begin to pray

161

And de angels of de Lawd locked de lion's jaw
Oh, wasn't dat a mighty day!
Good Lord, wasn't dat a mighty day!

The second and third stanzas reminded slaves of God's mighty deliverances in times past—the faithfulness of a mighty God to see His people through impossible situations. Bob and Linda faced more than one mountain. It seems they walked into a mountain range when the second cancer diagnosis came in, but through their faith in God's promises, they were able to travel their peaks and valleys and arrive at victory on the other side.

Regardless of where our feet rest, on our own mountain, valley, or somewhere in between, Bob and Linda's story reminds us that God is with us, every step of the way, and He will see us safely to the other side.

CHAPTER 33
SHEPHERD'S CROSSING

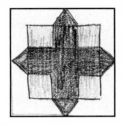

Dorene Lilley – Rochester Hills, Michigan

My Grandpa Haan, the son of Dutch Missionaries, enlisted in the U.S. Navy during World War II. His ship patrolled the Philippine coast just over a year before it was sunk near Iwo Jima by the Japanese. Grandpa survived the aftermath and returned stateside with post-traumatic stress disorder and alcohol addiction.

Grandma and Grandpa did not enjoy a happy marriage. Prior to Grandpa's enlistment, he and Grandma had four children, ages six months to eight years. My mother was six. Although Grandpa Haan was not gone long, the impact of his absence greatly affected his family. Mom tells few stories of her childhood and the ones she shares are of abuse, neglect and loneliness. As a teenager, she often worked after school in Grandpa's grocery, leaving little time to study or participate in extracurricular activities. At 17, she dropped out of school and met and married my dad.

My father, always a hard worker, put in long hours in the construction industry. He built our first house when I was a baby and later started a swimming pool company. My mother worked alongside him. The business did well, but Mom and Dad struggled in their marriage. Lacking a good example to follow, Mom only knew she should not follow in her mother's path and committed to restrain from venting her anger on her children. She made it her goal to be a good mom, but still battled loneliness and depression.

I was the oldest of the four children, followed by two brothers and a baby sister. We regularly attended church and my parents were involved in youth leadership. We went to catechism and Christian schools and had a good childhood, well provided for and loved, but a great sorrow entered October 19, 1971.

My brothers and sister played outside while I did my homework at the kitchen table. Mom needed to make a delivery, and as she stepped into the car to leave, four-year-old Suann ran to her. "Can I go?" she asked.

"Not now, your face is dirty," Mom said. "Just go play, and I will be right back." Suann rejoined my brothers in the front yard, and Mom began backing up. Unaware her daughter had darted from behind a bush to tell her something, Mom continued down the driveway.

Mom felt the car go over a bump. Certain she had run over a bike, she pulled forward so she could remove the obstacle and rolled over what she thought was a child's mangled toy a second time. When she stepped out of the car, panic exploded. She realized she had run over Suann—not once, but twice. Still at the kitchen table, I ran out to answer her call for help.

I knelt by my sister's body, and I remember singing softly to her. "Jesus loves you, this I know, for the Bible tells me so. Little ones to Him belong, they are weak but He is strong. Yes, Jesus loves you. Yes, Jesus loves you. Yes, Jesus loves you, the Bible tells me so." I felt angels nearby, both to comfort me and carry Suann to Heaven. That day, at the age of 12, I grew up.

Days melted together in a blur. My brothers and I went to friends' houses while arrangements were made. When we were home again, I clearly remember asking my dad "Where is she?"

Brokenly he answered, "Suann is in Heaven."

"No," I said. "Where is Mom?" I knew where Suann was, but I was afraid for my mother. She drifted in and out of reality, often asking me to find Suann, which I would pretend to do. In her despair, Mom became suicidal.

One day, as Mom woke up from a nap on the couch, she made an unusual request. "Dorene, go next door and get the preacher," she said. The preacher came, and she told him about a voice she had heard telling her to "be still." She wanted to know if she was going crazy. The preacher told her the Lord was speaking to her through

Psalm 46:10 "Be still and know that I am God." The realization that God truly cared about her was the first step toward Mom's healing. A friend invited her to join a Bible study, and she began her journey from grief as she moved forward in God's Word.

Our family joined a different church—one where we learned that God cared for us personally and we needed to invite Him into our lives. In his old age, Grandpa Haan became a Christian. As he lay dying of complications from a lifetime of smoking and drinking, he knew he was ready to go Home. "I see Pete," he said with a weak voice to everyone in his hospital room.

"St. Peter?" someone asked.

"Yes," he replied, "Him, too, but my brother, Pete! And I see Suann!" Praise God for a marvelous peek in Heaven's window.

For the most part, I was an obedient child. Rarely, beyond a little big-sisterly bossiness, did I go against my parents' wishes. I did not want to hurt my mom. But the summer after ninth grade, I lied to her about where I was going. Plans were in place to do something that night, something that almost landed me in dangerous trouble. From that experience, I realized my sinful ways and the severity of what could happen to me because of them. Conviction turned me to the Lord, and I asked Jesus for forgiveness. I realized I was not good enough to earn God's love and that the gift offered through Christ's death on the cross and His resurrection was free to me if I simply asked. I invited Him into my heart and life. Later that summer I attended Word of Life Camp and dedicated my life to God's service. I was baptized by immersion as a Christian in 1975.

Insecure and shy as a teen, I became more outgoing as God's love grew in me and what others thought lost its importance. Because of my mother's struggle with depression and our family history, I wanted to become a psychologist. I knew the answer to emotional problems was found in God's love, so I first enrolled in Bible school for a year to better understand His Word. Following, I attended Christian Heritage College (now San Diego Christian) in Southern California to study Biblical Psychology.

I became a Christian counselor to help those without hope find freedom in knowing Jesus. God keeps His promise to work all things out for good, even though at times we may feel lost in despair. I thank God for breaking the cycle of pain and addiction in my family and allowing my parents to raise their children under the guidance of God's Word.

Jesus promised in John 8:32, "Then you will know the truth, and the truth will set you free." By the grace of God, I am free, and very much looking forward to seeing Suann again someday.

❧ ❧

The Shepherd's Crossing quilt block dates at least as far back as the early 1900s. The design features four elongated hexagons that meet to form a cross. Matching squares in each corner, like little plots of pastureland, showcase the center design. Each block is set in a solid border, the points of the cross piercing through the border to the edge of the block.

Although not part of the "Quilt Code," the Shepherd's Crossing block brings to mind the beloved Psalm 23. Surely the men, women and children fleeing slavery's bonds sought the Lord's guidance as they walked through their "valleys" and sought "still waters" and "resting places" on their journeys. Many strong in faith leaned on the stabilizing staff of the Word as they faced adversity and adversaries alike.

I find one of the most beautiful aspects of the 23rd Psalm is the present tense in which it was written. With the words "Thou preparest a table before me," David implies that God ever prepares for his needs. A shepherd's "table," is set in high mountain country, the most sought after grazing land. Before releasing his sheep to pasture, a good shepherd prepares the table—examining vegetation, assessing dangers and removing poisonous plants.

Tragedies such as Dorene's household suffered often annihilate families—they just don't make it through the loss, the guilt, or the pain. But God prepared a table in her mother's dark valley. In the midst of suffering, He plucked out poisonous thoughts of suicide, mental anguish and potential bitterness and nourished her with His word. He called her to a place of rest in Him—the still waters of His presence.

The Lord is our shepherd. He knows our hurts and exactly how to reach into our hearts. The intersection of life and death, a family car and a precious little girl, became the path of the Shepherd's crossing in Dorene's family. Through the tragedy, He brought healing, salvation and hope into the lives of multiple generations. And He continues to pour out through Dorene as she ministers healing "oil" to hurting "sheep" through her Christian counseling practice. God does all things well and makes everything beautiful in His time.

The LORD is my shepherd; I shall not want.

He maketh me to lie down in green pastures:
he leadeth me beside the still waters.

He restoreth my soul: he leadeth me in the paths of righteousness
for his name's sake.

Yea, though I walk through the valley of the shadow of death,
I will fear no evil: for thou art with me;
thy rod and thy staff they comfort me.

Thou preparest a table before me in the presence of mine enemies:
thou anointest my head with oil; my cup runneth over.

Surely goodness and mercy shall follow me all the days of my life:
and I will dwell in the house of the LORD for ever.

"You will show me the path of life;
In your presence is fullness of joy;
At your right hand are pleasures forevermore"
(Psalm 16:11).

CHAPTER 34
FREEDOM

Jenny Teets – Farmingdale, New York

Although Costa Rica was a tropical paradise, a pleasant and peaceful country, in my memory it does not seem that way. The country's charm is not in question—it was undoubtedly a very beautiful place and that included the people, the food, the weather and even the language school which my husband and I attended. However, something bothered me terribly in Costa Rica; I have to admit that it surfaced in an unprecedented and undeniable fashion and rose to the top of my daily consciousness.

In spite of the fact that I was a mother of three, a minister's wife and supposedly mature enough to cope with life, I began to find I needed help in more areas of my life and soul than I had previously imagined. It was not our children I struggled with. They were my source of inspiration and pride. There were no issues between my husband and me; we were actually in the same situation. None of my friendships in Costa Rica were problematic; in fact, my friends supported me during that difficult time. What was it that bothered me so drastically in Costa Rica?

My great problem was that at 33 years of age, I had the humbling circumstance of becoming a beginner again in the language department. Being fluent in English, I can express myself in all situations, yet there I was in a foreign country unable to even buy a donut at the local grocery store. I had to submit myself to a level equal to a kindergarten class in the Spanish language. Having never lived in a foreign country before, I had not dealt with the difficulties and challenges of language barriers. I was frustrated and embarrassed.

The first step was to learn patience. As a grown adult, I was not accustomed to learning on such a basic level, or perhaps I should say I forgot how to be childlike in order to learn. I had become an important figure to many people, after all. I was an authority to my children. As a pastor's wife, I had counseled many people and had become a leader in several areas. Suddenly, and almost overnight, I had become just a number; all the status symbols with which I had become identified were yanked out from beneath me. I sat in a class with many other beginners who may have been doctors and lawyers by profession, now dethroned to become baby Spanish babblers beside me. It was a truly humbling realization that an average three-year-old in Costa Rica could understand and speak more of the language than we students could.

When faced (or forced) to learn a foreign language, I found it was most important to learn patience with myself. I have generally been the type of person who bravely accepts challenges, although I admit I have not always counted the cost of my endeavors before I tackled them. There is a fine line between having faith that things will work out and pacing oneself to live one day at a time. In my case, I had to find the right balance between studying one day at a time and keeping myself focused on my goals rather than my frustrations.

Looking back on my experience, the most important lesson I learned in Costa Rica was not about Spanish grammar. That was only a small part of the equation. The larger and more permanent lesson I learned was how to humble myself and become like a child; to become like a kindergartener in the learning process.

Kindergartners hold two basic attitudes which strike me as pretty smart. First, they humbly accept the courses laid out for them by their parents and teachers. Secondly, they take those courses one day at a time.

Amazingly, we rarely have to tell kids to be patient with themselves. It's as though in their general make-up they don't push themselves too hard. They don't label themselves as patient or impatient as adults do when they are in the learning process. They are excited with new experiences and learn impatience when adults introduce something called competition.

Humility is not a bad word. When we say, "that was humbling," we often mean we felt degraded by a situation, noticing the element of humility when we feel less important or less confident. True, there are times we are humbled without our consent. However, if we will humble ourselves and give our respect to another who has the greater rank—be it a school teacher, a pastor, or an official of any kind, we will do away with the pride that prevents us from truly learning.

To learn humility is to also learn the attitude of modesty. Often we encounter people who overwhelm us with braggadocio. They may even possess the abilities that they are boasting about, but listening to someone's self-praise and self-aggrandizement is sickening. Proverbs 27:2 says, "Let another man praise you, and not your own mouth; a stranger, and not your own lips." Modesty seems to be a forgotten virtue.

If adults are to become as kindergartners in new endeavors, they must also realize there is a lot to learn in "class"—a class that lasts a lifetime. On the first day of school, kindergartners have no concept of the many years of schooling that lie ahead of them. If they did, they might never enter the classroom. The humble, childlike attitude of "teacher knows more than I do" is one of the reasons a kindergartner can learn so easily. He will not be caught up in self-deprecation, self-pity or self-anything that might plague an adult. He will be too busy trying to conquer the tasks of reading and writing and math. His momentary fears will be just that—momentary. When he is discouraged, a simple pat on the back will be enough to encourage him once again.

I wonder what causes adults to be so fearful. When faced with the call to missions, I experienced many days of worry and fright. When I finally humbled myself to the call and prepared to leave for Costa Rica (one day at a time), amazingly, I gained a certain fortitude in the process. With the right attitude, I learned quickly and I was pleased when Spanish came easier to me than I had anticipated.

Since life is full of lessons to be learned, having teachers along the way is one of our greatest blessings. Becoming fluent in Spanish was achieved when I sat humbly in a classroom and learned Spanish from the native teachers. Imagine if we had to learn everything all on our own without any counsel, instruction or bits of wisdom from our elders. I cannot think of one discipline in grade school, high school or college I could have learned by myself, that is, without a teacher or professor guiding me towards the learning.

Jesus lived a life of humility. He was God, and yet He accepted a humiliating trial and public crucifixion. The grace, humility and patience of Jesus Christ with mankind are the most sterling virtues of a teacher we could ever know. His Word admonishes us to keep growing, "line upon line, precept upon precept" (Isaiah 28:10), or in other words, be patient with yourself; allow for continual growth, rather than strive for the fast growth. When we understand there will always be more to learn, it should compel us to become more Christlike in the learning process. When we wear the proper humility "mantle" of a life-long student, we are free to embrace the wonder of learning and growing, both in the natural and the spiritual.

A variety of Freedom quilt designs exist, many discussed in this book and included in the "Underground Railroad Quilt Code." Beyond traditional piecing and quilting methods, freedom quilting, or liberated quiltmaking, is a technique for those who want to "break out of the square" block patterns. Freestyle, free-hand piecing methods create lively, whimsical "blocks" that bring contemporary flavor to traditional patterns or often completely original, innovative designs. Liberated quilts are surprises in the making, "free spirited" quilts—the results of a process rather than a pattern.

Becoming a missionary in a foreign country, especially one where you do not know the language, is definitely "breaking out of the box." I admire people who invest so much of their lives responding to the call of God to serve in missions outreach. Jenny's transparent sharing of her struggle with the language barrier reaffirmed to me that missionaries are just everyday people God uses for His purposes. And, as with the freedom quilting technique, it does not seem to be important if your seams don't match or the points of your triangles are cut off just so. In liberated quiltmaking, you work on one section at a time, like the Scripture Jenny mentioned, line upon line, precept upon precept. In life, God does not always give a nice pattern or kit to follow, but we move where He, in His creative way, leads.

In freedom quilting, a mistake may turn out to be a masterpiece, the very focal point of the finished work. As Jenny learned to accept her situation and embrace the help she needed to communicate in a new language, she learned something new in God—a childlike attitude of humility.

God Almighty clothed Himself in humility when He, the King of all creation, wrapped His Spirit in human flesh and came to earth. The infant Jesus required diapering and burping, dependant on His creation to care for His every need. Just imagine!

As He grew, Jesus served others, even washing His disciples' feet. That is true humility, and an example we can learn from. We experience a new level of freedom when we embrace the fact that we do not know it all and, like Jesus, we give of ourselves to serve others.

"When life gives you scraps
make a quilt."

CHAPTER 35
NINE PATCH

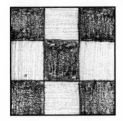

Lori Rose – Buford, Georgia

An unwanted, unplanned child of an unwed teen, my life was in jeopardy from its conception. I survived the hurdles of malnutrition, poverty and possible abortion and was adopted into a caring home. My parents loved and wanted me, but devastating abuse at the hand of a close relative caused my belief in their love to crumble at a very young age. With the perversion, I consumed a steady diet of lies about what kind of little girl I was. The harm I experienced, so I was told by my abuser, happened because of my wickedness. I believed it and wove my own web of lies to hide what was happening.

When I was 12, I had my first experience with God. My grandmother took me to church for a concert. The group used songs and skits and throughout the concert, I felt Jesus drawing my desperate heart. I did not understand what I felt, but I wanted to cry. Many of my friends went to the altar, but I gripped the pew in front of me until my knuckles turned white.

We left, and Grandma dropped me off at the lodge where my dad's band was playing. I planned to play a game of pool with friends, but I felt sick and had this feeling I was somewhere I should not be. I asked my mom for the car keys and went out to lie down in the back seat.

Once I shut the door, an overwhelming presence filled the car and I trembled at the power I felt. I felt so dirty and shameful and began to weep and moan. I had never cried like that. It lasted two hours, until my parents came out. I pretended to sleep, but once I got home and in my room, I asked God to forgive my sins and to do what He wanted in my life. I knew, somehow by faith, that this God was larger than any darkness and He could make me new.

The next day, I talked to a Sunday School teacher at the church. I told her I had asked Jesus to forgive me, come into my heart and save me, and I asked to be taught more about Him—how to really know God and have supernatural power to escape my darkness. She patted me on the head and said, "That's sweet." No one at the church could help me.

Unsure what to do, I called other churches. People gave me rides and I went from place to place trying to find what I felt that night at the concert. Unfortunately, my quest led me into more darkness. In the next three years, I found adults who knew about supernatural power and they schooled me in the powers of darkness. Without going into detail, I want to dispel any doubts about the reality of an organized satanic church complete with high "holy days." It is real, along with horrid rituals involving animals and people of all ages. I embraced it in my search to find God.

When I was 15, my friends and I cut an ad from the paper for a new youth center opening in Odessa. We took blood from our fingers and circled the ad. After incantations, I called the youth center and spoke with a young lady, Robin James. "Our beliefs are more powerful than yours," I told her. "You should close the youth center." To prove my point, I told her she was going to become sick and throw up, a result of our prayers.

"Oh, Jesus," she prayed with such compassion, "You see this young lady… and, Jesus, she needs You! I plead Your blood over her and over me, and I ask you to set her free."

I laughed and hung up, then instantly became nauseated and threw up. My friends left, clueless, but I knew what had happened. I felt the power of the One True Living God—Jesus! I grabbed the phone and dialed Robin again and asked, "How can I get what you have?"

Robin invited me to a street service at the college's student union building. Once on the campus, I watched a long time before I approached this odd looking group of people. Once I did, I was never the same. I came in direct contact with the one and only God. He filled me with the power of His Spirit and washed the stain of every sin from my soul. His supernatural power set me free from a world of self-deprecation, confusion, and pain.

I threw myself into serving God, only to feel shame again when, with good intentions and full of zeal, I made poor choices. At 17, I moved to Denver where Pastor Billy Hale invited me to live with his family, his wife, Brenda, and their two daughters. Melanie and Lori became like sisters to me and I love the Hales dearly. In their home, I grew in spiritual awareness and became anchored in the Word, yet I continued to make poor choices. It took years before I realized that even though God delivered me from the bondage of sin, I still believed the lies. In my mind, I was still that shameful little girl.

That lie was meant to destroy me. I had to find it, and replace it with truth. I was not shameful. I was an heir of salvation (Hebrews 1:14). I was carefully and wonderfully made (Psalm 139:14). God knew me in my mother's womb and the plans He had for me were for good and not evil (Jeremiah 29:11).

I discovered a great truth—one that changed my life forever. I learned to search out the core of my belief system and prove it. I replaced every lie with Truth, the Truth of God's Word and it has set me free. The desperation of abuse drove me to find a hero—someone to save me from my dark secrets and pain. My search led me to the only one who could truly help—Jesus, the Savior! Looking back, I can see so clearly that what Satan meant for evil, God used for good and He has given me a passion to share the liberating truth of freedom in Jesus with others. For me, the greatest purpose in life is to joyfully share this freedom, and in this, I am free indeed!

The Nine Patch square, though not associated with the "Quilt Code," connects in its own way with antebellum quilt designs, slavery, and freedom gained. Once fugitive slaves reached Canada, they provided backbreaking work clearing land. For their labor, the Canadian government allowed every man who cleared three acres to redeem one acre for himself. The newly freed men welcomed the opportunity to trade labor for land.

The Nine Patch quilt square is easy and endlessly versatile. The traditional block is made of nine squares equal in size sewn in three rows of alternating colors. The pattern is said to represent a "nine patch" garden planted by escaped slaves when they finally earned their acres of land as free men in a free country. It was a symbol of their liberty—they were truly free at last!

Mickey Mangun, the pastor's wife of Lori's former church, had this to say about Lori's journey to liberation. "Very few women overcome the early childhood abuse experiences Lori endured without forever being scarred and marred. The amazing thing about Lori is that though the road was a long and winding one, eventually she found a life in Christ that healed the pain of her past and directed her toward a future bright with hope. Hers is a story of amazing grace and the unmatched power of a life redeemed by and dedicated to Jesus Christ."

When I read Lori's story, I thought of the Nine Patch and how the efforts of liberated slaves to gain land for themselves resulted in an increase for others. Every "patch" Lori gained in her own growth and maturity with God, cleared ground for others. She works the fields with fervor, sharing the message of liberty and freedom from a grueling task master—the father of lies. When she learned the Truth of the Word, the truth of who she is in Christ, she experienced a liberty that now inspires others as Jesus shines through her bringing light into the darkness of those around her. Shine, Lori, shine!

CHAPTER 36
CUMBERLAND GAP

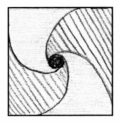

Claudette Walker – Oakland Township, Michigan

It's so easy to change the temperature in our our homes by simply readjusting the thermostat. Sometimes we allow the emotional thermostats of our marriages to change from positive to negative.

I remember one chilly fall evening this happened in my home. Marv and I had been married for six years and I was very upset with him. Since this happened 30 years ago, I can't remember exactly what I was upset about, but I do recall the evening well, and especially my method of coping.

I had recently read a magazine article that stated if you are very angry with a person, it is cathartic to write down the particular reasons the person upset you. I love to journal and so that appealed to me. I decided to give it a try. After six years of marriage, I finally had to face the facts—this man I was married to had some "real" problems. I got out my paper and pen and began to write the reasons Marv upset me.

Number One…He doesn't always polish his shoes on Saturay evening. My dad was president of Tupelo Children's Mansion, a pastor and our national Sunday School Secretary. Yet faithfully, every Saturday evening, he polished his big size 12 shoes. Marv only wore size 8-1/2. I thought surely he could find the time to polish his relatively small shoes.

Number Two…Most Tuesday evenings he forgot to carry the garbage out to the street. I could easily smell the week's buildup of stench in the garage. Why couldn't he? Of course, he would take it out after I reminded him, but please—couldn't he do it without having to be reminded? Give me a break! I told you the man had some "real" problems!

Quickly I wrote numbers three, four and five, then, when I tried to think of a sixth reason why Marv upset me, I drew a blank. Surely there were more than these five reasons after six years of marriage!

I was 29 years old and up to this point the Lord had never attended one of my "mad parties," but He did come to this one.

"Claudette," He called in His gentle voice.

"Yes, Lord?"

"Is there anything you like about Marv?"

"No. Not at the present moment. I'm upset with him!"

Because He's God and knows what is best, I knew what He was asking me to do. So I grumpily turned the paper over and thought really hard of a reason I liked him. When you have the em-PHA'sis on the wrong syl-LA'-ble in your marriage, you are scraping the bottom to think of the positive aspects of your mate.

Finally I wrote something down. Number One…He showers daily. After all, I would hate living with a stinky man!

Number Two…He works hard and provides well for our family.

I had to really think hard and force the thermostat of my heart from negative to positive for the first two reasons, but when I got to reason number three, all of a sudden things changed.

I saw a picture in my mind of Marv working in his office at home. Our two-year-old Jonathan walked up to his desk, a wiffle ball in one hand and a bat in the other. "Come on, Dad! Let's play ball."

Marv looked on his desk at all the work yet to do and into his son's pleading eyes then pushed his chair back away from the desk and went outside to play ball with his little boy. After Jonathan's slide into home plate, they gave each other high fives and jumped together for joy. The picture lingered, and I remembered how most times Marv did set aside his work and take a short break making time for our son.

OK. Number Three…He is a great father.

Quickly another picture came to mind. I saw Marv walking in the front door. Like so many other times he took one look and knew my solitary kidney was not working well. He gave me a big hug and said, "Honey, it will get better. Keep drinking lots of water. Put your feet up. I will go get some chicken from the Colonel tonight and then I will help you around here."

Never once in six years had he made me feel guilty because I was not always able to be on top of things at home. I cried as I wrote the fourth reason I loved Marv and thought, "Oh, what a wonderful man this is!"

When I got to the fifth, I saw us on vacation in Gatlinburg. We were Christmas shopping and I had to go into a lingerie shop to buy a gown for my dear friend, Jerolyn (Chambers) Kelly. She was getting married and I was her matron of honor. I saw a peach, lacy short gown and commented on how pretty it was. Very ready to leave the lingerie store, Marv said, "Good. Get it and let's go."

I told him Jerolyn would not like that gown. I liked it. Finally, I found a pretty blue one for her. The next day, as we were packing up to leave our motel, I looked in the bag and there was the peach gown. When I told Marv the clerk had packaged the wrong gown, he smiled and said, "No, she didn't. I went back later and got it for you. I hope you had a fun vacation." I started to cry as I wrote Number Five. "Oh, how I love this wonderful man!"

I wrote as fast as I could, tears dripping on my paper all the way to Number 24. I stopped there—not because I couldn't think of any more reasons why I loved my husband, but because I knew it was time to repent.

"Oh, Lord, please forgive me for putting the em-PHA'-sis on the wrong syl-LA'-ble, and letting the thermostat in my heart go from positive to negative. Thank you for my dear husband and help me be to him the wife I need to be."

"Claudette," came the Lord's gentle whisper in my heart. Repentant, submissive and eager now to hear, I answered, "Yes, Lord?"

"If it is such a big deal to you that Marv's shoes are polished every Saturday night, then why don't you just polish them yourself?"

That story happened 30 years ago, and since then I have made lots of mistakes in my marriage, but never again concerning his shoes. I bought every color of polish, an electric buffer and heel dressings.

Every time I polish his shoes I remember how very easy it is to focus on the negative aspects of our spouses—how very easy it is to put the em-PHA'-sis on the wrong syl-LA'-ble. As I polish his shoes, I thank God for my wonderful husband.

How long has it been since you made a list of all the wonderful qualities you love in your mate? That long? Go get pen and paper or sit at your computer. I promise you if you will put your hand on the emotional thermostat of your marriage, the Lord Jesus will put his hand over yours and help you turn the dial from the negative to the positive. Although this exercise may cost you a lifetime of shoe polishing, it can also free you from a heart full of bitterness.

❧

The Cumberland Gap quilt pattern is a multi-patch design, a four-sided shape as a piece. The pattern represents the natural break in the Appalachian Mountains, the pass located just north of where Kentucky, Tennessee and Virginia meet. Also known as the "Gateway to the West," the Cumberland Gap is the chief passageway through the Central Appalachians and part of two famous routes: the Wilderness Road traveled by pioneers settling the west, and the Underground Railroad traveled by runaway slaves seeking freedom in the north. Slaves from the deep south states of Alabama and Georgia, as well as Tennessee, traveled the Underground Railroad through the 12 mile opening into Kentucky, Ohio and ultimately Ontario hiding in caves along the way.

During the Civil War, both Union and Confederate armies fought for the Cumberland Gap. Remains of earthworks mark the fortifications and battle lines of great clashes of humanity that took place around the pass.

Although our interpersonal relationships lack the visible trenches and peaks of earthworks fortifications, battleground posturing is often evident in our attitudes and reactions to others—invisible wounds and scars marking the emotional terrain.

For runaway slaves, completing the pass from one side of the Cumberland Gap to the other meant liberty. Undoubtedly, at the beginning of the 12-mile trek the goal seemed distant, difficult or perhaps even unachievable. As we deal with the relationships in our lives, especially those closest to us, sometimes the chasms seem insurmountable, but as Claudette shared, a change in attitude, a purposeful turning of the emotional "thermostat," can bridge the gap and bring deliverance to a mind trapped in the captivity of wrong thinking.

When she was nine, my daughter asked me if a person can change their own attitude. Claudette's story instantly came to mind. "Yes, you can," I answered with confidence. "By choosing to look on the positive instead of the negative." Regardless of the situation, we can find something positive to focus on if we make the choice to do so. And if our struggles cloud finding something good in this life to think about, we can open the Word and read about God's wonderful gifts of forgiveness and grace—and our promise of a glorious future in heaven with the best spouse ever—Jesus! When this life leaves us empty or hurting, we can still thank God for the bridge of the cross and that through His sacrifice and our positive response to it through repentance, baptism and being born of the Spirit, God's "list" on you and me flips from "sinner" to "saint." One day we will cross the great divide between natural and supernatural, mortality and immortality and walk in the land of true liberty forever. Now that is something to be thankful for!

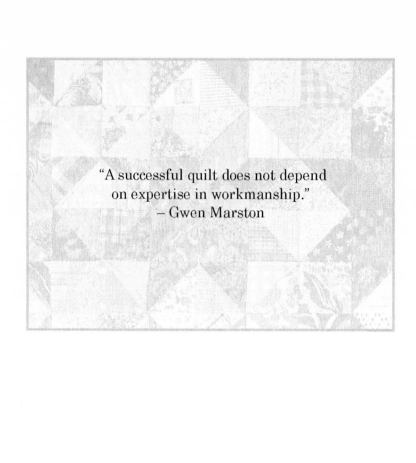

"A successful quilt does not depend
on expertise in workmanship."
— Gwen Marston

Chapter 37
RING OF ROSES

Lydia Gagoh – Rochester Hills, Michigan

I was teaching in Manchester, England at the time, and one particular Monday, the atmosphere of antagonism in my eleventh grade science class grew denser by the minute. Lakisha and Jayden hurled insults at each other to the amusement of the rest of the students while I stood at the front of the class wondering what sparked the heated argument.

"Will you please stop the name calling or you will both be punished," I said raising my voice slightly.

Lakisha responded immediately, but Jayden carried on, spewing more offensive words. I knew reasoning would have been a waste of time and in the midst of Jayden's tirade, I interjected, "Fine! See me for detention after school!"

Jayden became enraged and turned on me, calling me every name he could think of. I was stunned. Two previous disciplinary experiences had left me with permanent scars: once when I was hit several times in the head trying to break up a fight, and another when I was shoved during my first pregnancy.

The bell rang for lunch and I was able to keep Lakisha behind as the rest of the students exited. She explained that the argument began when people made fun of Jayden about something he said. I talked to her about her behavior, took a moment to compose myself and reported the incident.

On the way home that afternoon, I met Mr. Jackson, the Deputy Head. He acknowledged receipt of the report, but to my surprise,

185

seemed to excuse Jayden's behavior saying Jayden had recently experienced a family bereavement. This annoyed me considerably and I told him that was no reason to condone his disrespectful behavior in the classroom. Mr. Jackson assured me the matter would be addressed and he would keep me informed.

Being a part-time science teacher, I missed Tuesday and returned the following morning. As I stood by the photocopier waiting to make copies for my classes, one of the teachers joined me. "Lydia, did you hear what happened to Jayden?"

"No." I replied.

"He was given a one-day detention. They were careful not to contact home because of some family issues."

I looked at her in surprise. "Mr. Jackson said he was going to contact me about the incident."

"When I spoke to Mr. Jackson, he said he had sent you an e-mail."

"An e-mail!" I was shocked.

"Oh, I'm sorry. I shouldn't have said anything," she said when she saw my reaction.

All of a sudden, I felt grief stricken. Betrayed and disappointed, I broke down and cried. I was ushered to a private room and later led to the principal's office. While I sat there, still crying, Mr. Jackson walked in. He saw me and left without a word. That only upset me further.

When the Head, Mr. Cox arrived in the office, I shared the details of the incident with him and told him I did not want Jayden in my class ever again. "That's not possible," he said, telling me that was not in line with school ethos. I was left feeling numbed, with a sense of injustice, questioning my treatment—that perhaps it was because I was black, or because Jayden was.

The senior deputy, Mrs. Smith, walked into the office. She seemed more sympathetic and comforted me with the strangest words. "Lydia, why don't you go home and do something you enjoy. I know you like to sing."

I laughed, thinking she must be joking. A pity party seemed the more appropriate response, but I took her advice. Somehow the seed Mrs. Smith planted settled into my spirit. I went to a community center to spend time with my friends and found comfort in the studio singing and listening to music.

Later that evening, in prayer, the Lord graciously helped me choose to forgive Jayden as well as the school authorities, including Mr. Jackson. The Lord changed my perspective by showing me that His love in action was the key in this situation. This revelation gave me compassion towards Jayden and Mr. Jackson. Pain had blinded my ability to see, but grace opened my horizon.

When I returned to school, I felt vulnerable, but God strengthened me. Jayden was not in class for two weeks, then one morning his tutor informed me he was returning to class.

Jayden was brought in to see me and said he was very sorry for his behavior. I accepted his apology, expressing that my heart's desire was to see him succeed in every area of his life. The short time of sharing face to face was significant. As we spoke, I felt God's compassion and love flowing from me towards Jayden.

Jayden apologized in front of the class and normal and relations were reestablished. Jayden's behavior improved and I noticed the rest of the students were more mindful about their conduct as well.

Talking to Mr. Jackson remained a challenge. We greeted one another in the halls, but we never mentioned the incident again.

One morning, I woke up feeling God's encouragement to thank Mr. Jackson for allowing me to grow through the situation with Jayden. I was at peace and ready to obey knowing that Proverbs 3:5-6, NIV, says, "Trust in the LORD with all your heart and lean not on your own understanding; in all your ways acknowledge him, and he will make your paths straight."

At the first opportunity, I acknowledged to Mr. Jackson I had been hurt by how the incident had been handled, but wanted to thank him because God used the situation to make me stronger. He smiled, but said little. Walking away, I felt the freedom of forgiveness and the victory of walking in God's love.

The Ring of Roses, a medallion quilt also known as the Presidential Wreath, served as a type of laurel wreath in the days of slavery—a symbol of victory. Although the pattern was not used along the Underground Railroad, author Clarice Boswell indicates the quilt was given to families arriving safely at the end of the line. In a February 2005 interview with *Kentucky Living Magazine*, Boswell, a Kentucky native who learned quilt code secrets from her grandmother, indicated the Ring of Roses held special significance to her. "Whenever I see them give the roses to the horse who wins the Kentucky Derby," Boswell said, "I think of the Ring of Roses quilt, which represented a celebration of life."

Most of us have seen pictures of championship horses blanketed with roses. The famed Kentucky Derby is nicknamed "Run for the Roses," and I believe that is what Lydia was sharing in her story, her own personal quest for victory.

Lydia is a thoroughbred—a woman of fine character and an excellent spirit. I can't imagine her raising her voice in a classroom, although I'm sure she did not fabricate her story. We all "lose it" from time to time, but God is gracious. He shows us ourselves in a reflection of His grace-in-action in our lives and He helps us extend His mercy and forgiveness to those who hurt or disappoint us.

Jayden may never have asked forgiveness, and Mr. Jackson did not respond the way Lydia hoped, but Lydia was free when she allowed the compassion and love of God to work forgiveness in her heart. And real victory came when she shared her liberty, the freedom of forgiveness, first with Jayden and then Mr. Jackson. Roses worn by a championship thoroughbred share their sweet fragrance with horse and rider alike. Jayden and Mr. Jackson both enjoyed the scent of Lydia's victory. As we face our own conflicts, I hope we will remember Lydia's example and choose to "run for the roses."

CONTRIBUTING AUTHOR BIOGRAPHIES

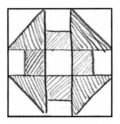

Teresa Altman (Crossroads), a divorced mother of two and proud grandmother of six, lives in rural northwest Tennessee. After working as an engineer for 25 years, she answered God's call to write in 2007. She is a member of FaithWriters and finds inspiration to write from her relationship with Jesus Christ and His unconditional devotion to her.

Troy Butler (The Big Dipper) is an advocate for people with disabilities and a peer mentor for a local agency where people with physical disabilities receive services. He has shared his life story, "Count it all Joy: My Life Journey with God" in book form available through Rochester College, contact Cathy Rise, crise@rc.edu or by phone (248) 218-1201.

Dustin-Lee Casey (Underground Railroad) is a part-time student living in Nebraska. He has written for various Christian blogs and websites over the past few years and is currently working on his first novel. In his spare time he has designed several Christian websites. His personal blog is www.dustin-lee.com.

Lynnette Countaway (Dresden Plate) is a minister's wife and a registered dental hygienist. The Countaways, pastored in Albany, New York, and now live in Paw Paw, Michigan, where they attend Full Gospel Apostolic Church. Lynnette is a youth Sunday school teacher and home group leader. She is an active soul winner and involved in many other areas of ministry. Lynnette enjoys gardening and writing and aspires to eventually publish a book. She lives with her husband, William and their adored pets, Bella & Chloe.

Janine Dunlop (Bear's Paw) has worked at Wayne State University for 31 years. She enjoys reading, cooking and helping others. Janine and her husband Karl, live in Warren, Michigan. They have 2 children, Craig age 22, and Jennifer age 17, and a poodle named Tara.

Pam English (Flying Geese) is the wife of Ron, mother of two, William and Mary, and "gram" of three beautiful grandchildren, Benny III, Marisa and Marley. She lives in Rochester Hills, MI with her husband. She enjoys scrapbooking, having tea with friends, and playing with her grandchildren. She is a full-time caregiver to an elderly couple, and has three house cleaning jobs per week.

Lydia Gagoh (Ring of Roses) lives in Rochester, Michigan, with her husband Oscar, their two sons Joshua 10 and Ese 8, and their twin baby girls, Hannah and Olivia. As a writer, speaker and singer, her passion is to spread the Gospel of Jesus to the nations by sowing seeds of encouragement. To get in touch: email: Lydgagoh@hotmail. com or visit www.beautifulandhighlyfavored.blogspot.com

Claudia Gajewski (Stars) is a wife, mother, writer and scrapbooker. She loves to help people capture their stories and memories in meaningful ways. A lifelong Catholic, Claudia rejoices with her interdenominational friends, neighbors, family and customers who show God's love every day. She can't wait to clean out her attic and start quilting American quilts!

Constance Gilbert (Morning Glory) retired, after 45 years of nursing, ready for her new God assignment. First, she became a gramma. Then her childhood dream to be a writer became a reality at age 60. Connie says, "I had to wait for cyber space to connect me to the world." As the editor for *4Him2U*, writer of a bi-monthly column for *Positively Feminine,* and editing several e-books due out this year, her gray cells stay stimulated. But to be sure, she studies Hebrew and reads mysteries. Her short stories have found homes in several anthologies and she is writing her first non-fiction book.

Chris Gueydan (Tumbling Blocks) earned an Associates of Science in Business Technology and a Bachelor of General Studies form Louisiana Tech University. He holds a Master of Divinity from Wesley Biblical Seminary. Chris is a member of First Pentecostal Church, Jackson, where he is active in motorcyclist outreach and Boy Scouting. He is an Ambassador and First Connect Volunteer for recently diagnosed cancer patients with the Leukemia Lymphoma Society. Chris became a Chaplain Resident at G. V. (Sonny) Montgomery VA Medical Center in February 2008. He and his wife Donya have four sons and live in Raymond, Mississippi.

Jacquelin Harris (Catch Me If You Can) and her husband Thomas live in Englewood, Ohio. She is a homemaker and mother of two wonderful sons, Tj, who is in the US Air Force and Chad, who is studying electronics engineering. Her family has lived in several states as well as England. She has enjoyed writing for the local church newsletters and "Today's Apostolic Woman" magazine.

David Hepworth (Wagon Wheel) is a pastor, singer/songwriter, and a technician in a catheterization lab at a large Michigan hospital. He is a husband and father of six. He and his wife desire most to see each of their children walk with the Lord.

Cynthia Khan (Bow Ties) was born in Pakistan. She has served as the Staff Director of Ethnic Ministries for Faith Lutheran Church in Troy, Michigan, and has a passion to love and minister to Muslim women. She is currently involved in a new venture to bring Christ to the nations community outreach through 24-hour Christian programming on Yahweh TV (www.yahtv.org). Cynthia also teaches a cooking class at Macomb Community College.

Dorene Lilley (Shepherd's Crossing) is a full-time mom of three teens, and a licensed therapist in Rochester Hills, Michigan. She writes a monthly advice column in The Woodside News under the pseudonym, O. Kaye. She can be reached at www.keycounseling.com.

Anne Linington (Bird in the Air) lives in the United Kingdom, and attends an evangelical Church of England, where she is training as a Reader,(lay preacher). She supports the work of a Christian Healing Centre, and enjoys writing, particularly poetry.

Carol McCartney (Courthouse Steps) like most women today, finds herself filling a number of roles: child of God, wife (married to Bruce for 37 years; mother of two adult children; grandmother; daughter; sister; business woman; student; MOPS Mentor; neighbor and friend. At mid-life Carol considers herself a "student of life" and has pursued university studies with a focus on philosophy, psychology, and anthropology. She is also a serious student of the Bible and feels one may learn from every individual encounter...especially those encounters with individuals between 3-5 years of age. Carol is always ready and eager to share her life experiences, as she firmly and passionately believes God allows events, situations, and people into our lives for a reason...that He may be glorified through all and in all.

Anne McManus (Sailboat) is a liturgical dancer and choreographer. She has co-directed a girls praise dance choir at her church and been a soloist for worship, conferences and retreats. While not a writer, Anne is blessed to be part of this collection, and receives comfort and inspiration from God's gift of memory. Anne and her husband, Walter, live in Rochester Hills, Michigan. They have two grown children and a black Lab named Maxwell.

Terry Michaels (Drunkard's Path) is a pastor at Calvary Chapel of the Springs in San Marcos, Texas. He was a radio personality in the 70s and 80s but finds greater fulfillment serving God's people. He has two daughters and lives with his wife of 29 years, Christy, in the Texas Hill Country. He is author of 'That I May Know You' which is his first book. www.terrimichaels.org

Val Mossop (Monkey Wrench) lives in Surrey, British Columbia, with her husband of 46 years. She has a passion for writing and in that capacity is editing "Writers' Corner" for her local Seniors Center. Deaf Ministry in the church is her other passion and she has been involved for many years.

Susan Paurazas (Log Cabin) lives in Rochester Hills, Michigan. She is an endodontist who practices part-time and teaches at the University of Detroit Mercy. She enjoys the creative process of writing and has been published in an anthology of poetry, and Chicken Soup for the Dental Soul. She is thankful to her husband and daughter for their enthusiastic support.

LaNaye Perkins (Lost Children) From the beginning the Lord let LaNaye know she was to share whatever He inspired her to write. Now, over a decade later, she's still sharing what He's given. "Blessed be God, Who comforteth us in all our tribulation, that we may be able to comfort them which are in any trouble, by the comfort wherewith we ourselves are comforted of God" (2 Corinthians 1:3-4 KJV). Every time she goes through a trial, she gets a burning desire to write of it, so she can encourage others with the same comfort God gives her.

Debbie Roome (Basket) was born and raised in Zimbabwe and spent 15 years in South Africa before moving to New Zealand with her husband and 5 children. She now works as a freelance writer and her work has been published in several countries and extensively on the internet. Her main passion is writing stories that touch people's lives and point them to God.

Lori Rose (Nine-Patch) the single mother of three adult children, has spent years winning souls and teaching others the wisdom in doing the same. A teacher of soul winning seminars, a public speaker, and an amateur writer, Lori always refers back to her roots in Odessa, Texas, under Pastor J.T. Pugh, but calls Landmark Tabernacle of Denver, Colorado, home. In 2007, she moved to Georgia and attends First Pentecostal Church of Oakwood with Pastor Alan and Sister Denise Stewart. www.LorisMusings.com

Dr. Helen Roseveare (Bright Hopes) served as an English Christian missionary from 1953-1973 pioneering vital medical work in the rain forests of the Belgian Congo, later known as Zaire and currently the Democratic Republic of the Congo. After Independence in 1964, the country was ravaged by the Simba Rebellion. Dr. Roseveare, caught up in the horror of the revolution, was beaten, raped and imprisoned by the rebels. After several months, she escaped, and after a year's recovery, returned again to the mission field. Dr. Roseveare has had a worldwide ministry in speaking and writing. Now retired, she lives in Northern Ireland. Her life of service was portrayed in the 1989 film Mama Luka Comes Home. She has written several books: He Gave Us A Valley, Give Me This Mountain, Living Sacrifice: Willing to be Wittled Like an Arrow, Digging Ditches: The Last Chapter of an Inspirational Life available at www.amazon.com.

LauraLee Shaw (Independence Square) "A disciple of Jesus Christ disguised as a wife, mom and writer"—this is how LauraLee wants her life to be defined. Her heart's desire is for Jesus to be the One identified in each and every role to which God calls her. You can sign up for her edevos and short story fiction pieces athttp://www.lovinthearts.com or visit her ministry blog daily at http://lovinthearts.blogspot.com.

Kimberly Sciscoe (Shoofly) is a wife, mother, author and speaker. She has ministered as a schoolteacher, pastor's wife and most importantly—as an active soul winner. She and her husband Jason and daughter Julianna live in Dallas, Texas, and evangelize both domestically and internationally. For contact information, bookings and other empowering resources visit the web site at www. triumphtoday.org.

Karen Skolney (Maple Leaf) is married to a wonderful husband, and has four beautiful children who are all homeschooled. She and her family enjoy the outdoors and family gatherings. They reside on acreage near Kelvington in Saskatchewan. Karen enjoys writing inspirational poetry and one day hopes to publish a book of poetry.

Susan Snover (Double Wedding Ring) is a home school mother for the first time and is enjoying the time she has to teach and shape her son into who God wants him to be. In her spare time she makes beautiful cards to share with others, and enjoys poetry, especially writing it. Although she is still a bit shy she tries to follow where God leads, like singing in the choir and reading her poetry in public. Susan is very blessed to be a part of this book, and having the opportunity to share her story with you. Susan and Her Husband, Richard, live in Hazel Park, Michigan. They have four Children.

Maria Spencer (Cats and Mice) and her family reside in Poland, Ohio. She and her husband Michael are the parents of two, Jonah and Olivia. Olivia is a person with hemipelegic cerebral palsy. Because of her experiences with Olivia, Maria provides parent-to-parent support for families involved in her local early intervention program. Her gift for writing has come directly from the Lord since Olivia's diagnosis. She writes a monthly column entitled, "Special Parents, Special Kids" for the Mahoning Valley Parent magazine in Ohio. She is also a contributing author at www.mommiesmagazine.com, and writes a weekly blog at www.thenarrowgateinvites.blogspot.com. Maria is very passionate about getting the word out to special parents that they are not alone in their journey of raising their special child; and that they were chosen by God to parent their children. She welcomes comments and questions at sri19952000@yahoo.com.

Jenny Teets (Freedom), born to Victor and Theodora Jordan in Indianapolis, Indiana, always wanted to become a teacher, but instead became the wife of a minister, and eventually the mother of four children. She and her husband pastored in three successive churches before serving as missionaries in Uruguay, South America. After their return to the States, Jenny's husband was appointed as the coordinator of the New York Metro District of the United Pentecostal Church where he served as Superintendent for 12 years and Jenny served as the Ladies Division president for 13 years. The couple has pastored the New Life Apostolic Church, Ozone Park, New York, since 1986. Jenny finished her college degree at Queens College (CUNY) with a BA/MA in Philosophy and was elected into the Alpha Sigma Lambda sorority in her senior year. After graduation, she wrote *Married to Ministry,* available through the Pentecostal Publishing House catalog, and is presently working on a second book about missions. http://ozonemusings.squarespace.com/

Bill Wagner (Britches II) runs his own drywall, plaster and stucco business in Rochester Hills, Michigan. He is actively involved in many areas of ministry at Faith Apostolic Church of Troy and has recently become certified as a chaplain through First Responders Chaplain Association. He and his wife, Lori, have four children and one spoiled dog.

Bob and Linda Welch (Going Around the Mountain) make their home in Warren, Michigan. They are the parents of two wonderful adult children who have blessed them with two amazing grandaughters. They have a son-in-law and daughter-in-law that are precious to them and are loved like their own. Bob and Linda both pray their testimonies will encourage those going through catastrophic illnesses to keep their focus on Jesus and trust Him to take them through the valley of despair, looking for the blessings along the way. Bob and Linda both serve in various ministries at Zion Christian Church where they try to help God's people grow in His amazing love.

Bonnie Winters (Butterfly) is the author of a biblical novel, Daughter of Lot, available through major online booksellers. She writes a monthly column called "Patches of Grace" for 4Him2U. com and has authored devotionals, articles on abuse and recovery, children's ministry ideas, short stories and drama. As a pastor's wife with over 30 years of ministry experience, she is involved in women's ministry, music and children's ministry. Bonnie is a graduate of the Institute of Pastoral Counseling through Emerge Ministries, Akron, Ohio; Zion Bible College in Barrington, Rhode Island, and SUNY Empire State College, Binghamton, New York. Visit Bonnie online at http://inkitblog.blogspot.com.

Don Wisler (Crossing Ohio) has been married to Tam for 38 years. They live in Dublin, Ohio, and have four grown children and two grandchildren. Don has been a social worker for over 35 years and is currently the CEO of Catholic Social Services in Columbus, Ohio.

Kim Zaksek (Beacon Light) currently lives in northeastern Ohio with her husband and three children. Kim has a heart for missions and a burden to make a difference for Christ for those the world abuses, forgets, ignores or abandons. She has traveled internationally to pursue that call on her life. She also has a heart for adoption. You can find more of her writing on thenarrowgateinvites.blogspot.com.

NOTES/RESOURCES

Brackman, Barbara. Encyclopedia of Pieced Quilt Patterns.
American Quilter's Society, Paducah, KY. 1993.

Burns, Eleanor and Sue Bouchard. Underground Railroad Sampler.
Quilt in a Day, Inc., San Marcos, CA. 2003.

Tobin, Jacqueline L. and Raymond G. Dobard, Ph. D. Hidden in
Plain View; A Secret Story of Quilts and the Underground
Railroad. Anchor Books, New York, NY. 1999.

http://www.kentuckyliving.com/article.asp?articleid=1343&issueid
=233. Clarice Boswell in KY shares Lizzie's version of the
quilt code.

Sources: http://ses.westport.k12.ct.us/squire/idivsquares.
htm#The%20Underground%20Railroad%20Quilt

http://www.patternsfromhistory.com/colonial_revival/dresden-
plate.htm